"IRREVERENT, PUNKY ROCKERS WITH A JONES FOR RHYTHM AND BLUES VERNACULAR, both lyrical and musical, and a commitment to humor, variety, and unbridled stylistic independence."
—Rolling Stone

"THE ABSOLUTE FUNK-ROCK MATRIX."
—Interview Magazine

"The pummeling 'Give It Away' and the incendiary 'Suck My Kiss' established a template for rock punctuated by the beatcentric relentlessness of hip-hop that would be appropriated by everyone from Limp Bizkit to Dr. Dre."
—Rolling Stone

"Accessible successors of P-Funk."
—All Music Guide

"Stadium Arcadium is a mature showcase of concentrated power with riotous groove jams, super-sized hooks and transcendent vocal arrangements...One wild melodic rush...the message is loud and clear: twenty-three years into their career, THE RED HOT CHILI PEPPERS SOUND EUPHORIC AND ENORMOUSLY ALIVE."
—Billboard Magazine

"One Hot Minute is a FEROCIOUSLY ECLECTIC AND IMAGINATIVE disc that also presents the band members as more thoughtful, spiritual—even grown-up. After a 10 plus-year career, they're realizing their potential at last... Now their belief in the power of jamming, innovation and spontaneity is fully unleashed."
—Rolling Stone

"OVERFLOWS WITH THE KIND OF MUSIC THE CHILI PEPPERS DO BEST: a physical, often psychedelic mix of spastic bass-slapped funk and glistening alt-rock spiritualism. Only they've never sounded this good as musicians."
—L.A. Times

RED HOT CHILI PEPPERS:

IN THE STUDIO

RED HOT CHILI PEPPERS:

IN THE STUDIO

By Jake Brown

Colossus Books
Phoenix
New York   Los Angeles

RED HOT CHILI PEPPERS
IN THE STUDIO

By Jake Brown

Published by:
Colossus Books
A Division of Amber Communications Group, Inc.
1334 East Chandler Boulevard, Suite 5-D67
Phoenix, AZ 85048
Amberbk@aol.com
WWW.AMBERBOOKS.COM

Dedication

This book is dedicated to some of my favorite Thieme women, who in my opinion don't always get the acknowledgment they deserve. For their resilience over the last couple of trying years, for our broader family, and in the process—for illustrating why real family ties are woven so tightly:

Heather Ann (you deserve BIG NODS) for all you have given of your heart and time over the past few years to Grammie, first and foremost, our lovely cousins Erin and Emily, your sister Vickie last spring, and Papa more recently; as well as for keeping that lovely smile and spirit of yours—even in your own times of trouble. You inspire me all the time…

My Aunt Debbie, for all the dedication you've put in over the years looking after Papa (and ME re VR, ☺) I'm grateful always to your uplifting energy, outlook, and wonderful life advice.

My Auntie Vickie, congrats first off to fully recovering from your horrible ordeal last spring; it stopped time for all of us. I'm happy life is moving ahead so healthily for you. Next for what you did for Gram, and congratulations on Erin's beautiful wedding… and for doing such a lovely job raising her and Emily; they are both precious young women.

Finally, to my creative muse and mother, Christina Lee Thieme-Brown. You're artistically—among MANY other reasons—a KEY to why the world keeps turning my way and opening up such wonderful doors for me professionally, so thank you. Also, since you also started letting me listen to this band when I was 11, and I have been a fan ever since, thank you for that freedom as a child to be uninhibited in my musical travels! It paid off, for me anyway.

Contents

Red Hot Chili Peppers Debut
1983

Freakey Styley
1985

The Uplift Mofo Party Plan
1987

Mother's Milk
1989

Blood/Sugar/Sex/Magik
1991

One Hot Minute
1995

Californication
1999

By the Way
2002

Stadium Arcadium
2006

Introduction

The Red Hot Chili Peppers
in the Studio

According to one leading astronomer, "gold...platinum and other exotic heavy elements forged in the explosions of massive stars are leading the way to understanding the birth of elements in our Milky Way." As often as rock 'n' roll and astrology are analogized, one band shines brighter than most in highlighting why. The astral sky of the Red Hot Chili Peppers' musical universe is dotted with as many million of stars as records they've sold and fans they've collected in their 25-year odyssey. Among music's larger universe, the brilliant collage of living musical colors created by Anthony Kiedis, Flea, John Frusciante, and Chad Smith, as well as founding members Hillel Slovak and Jack Irons, will be admired, studied, musically marveled over, and referenced derivatively by bands for generations to come.

Embodying a musical imagination without stylistic inhibitions or boundaries, the band's sound was erotic, spontaneous, resonant, wildly melodic, musically sophisticated, boundlessly energetic, beautifully funky, groundbreaking, trend setting, and always futuristic. The core to understanding the creative essence of the Red Hot Chili Peppers is to explore the science behind their creative process—a voyage we begin in the pages of *The Red Hot Chili Peppers: In the Studio*. Tracing through *The Red Hot Chili Peppers* (1983), *Freaky Styley* (1985), *The Uplift Mojo Party Plan* (1987), *Mother's Milk* (1989), *BloodSugarSexMagik* (1991), *'One Hot Minute* (1995), *Californication* (1998), *By the Way* (2002), and *Stadium Arcadium*

(2006), we see that there isn't a musically stylistic frontier that the Chili Peppers haven't mastered and always surpassed. While we can't know the full impact of the band's ultimate influence on rock—as their legacy is far from concluded—at the end of this story, fans will have an intimate understanding of a band inarguably among rock's most potent and timeless stars and sounds.

The masters of melding melody with madness, the Red Hot Chili Peppers are a musical kaleidoscope—blending funk with every conceivable subgenre of popular music, sending listeners on a rock 'n' roll roller coaster where every turn offers a new musical revelation and concept. Consider Flea's definition of the band's sound: "the Red Hot Chili Peppers have never been a part of any movement or any collective thing or any existing category. We just try to create our own categories." Playing with the passion of a first kiss among soul mates, the Chili Peppers were always as brilliant individually as they were in sum musically, mainstreaming funk-rock, rap-rock, punk-pop, melodic art-rock, hip-hop, as well as undoubtedly a plethora of future rock subgenres that we haven't even popularly discovered yet into one cohesive work. Allmusic.com's summary of the band's influence concludes, "Few rock groups of the '80s broke down as many musical barriers and were as original as the Red Hot Chili Peppers. Creating an intoxicating new musical style by combining funk and punk rock together with an explosive stage show, to boot, the Chili Peppers spawned a slew of imitators in their wake, but still managed to be the leaders of the pack by the dawn of the 21st century." According to long-time producer Rick Rubin, "they're very different individuals. Each has their own world."

Part I
Roots of the Red Hot Chili Peppers

The Childhood of
Anthony Kiedis and Flea

The Red Hot Chili Peppers have symbolized the true eclecticism of Hollywood for better than a quarter-century. Though in their musical personality as a band, according to Flea, the band reflected L.A. "to the bone," core members Anthony Kiedis and Flea each began their journey far removed from the sunny coast of Southern California. For lead singer/lyricist Anthony Kiedis, life began on November 1, 1962 in Grand Rapids, Michigan. He was the love child of hippie parents John Kiedis and Margaret 'Peggy' Idema, who divorced when Anthony was just three years old. Kiedis' father John moved to California shortly after that, while the infant stayed living in Michigan with his mother, who soon remarried. The remarriage produced a brood of siblings, including two sisters, Julie and Jenny, and a brother James, with whom Kiedis remained close even as he took more and more frequent trips to visit his father in Los Angeles. At age 11, Kiedis had moved to Los Angeles to live full-time with his father, an aspiring actor, local celebrity, and regular at the legendary Rainbow Room who went by the screen name Blackie Dammett and regularly socialized with the members of Led Zeppelin and the Who among others.

In junior high and high school Anthony was surrounded by the rock 'n' roll lifestyle. Anthony began experimenting with narcotics just out of grade school and would remain addicted to heroin until the late 1990s. Still, in reflecting back on the roots of his long-term addiction, Kiedis quickly defends his father:

I don't think my dad knew any better…He was just going, 'Look what I found, this is fun, this is wonderful, let's do it together.'…During that time, everyone wanted to turn everyone on to it, no one knew how bad it was…No one had really figured out that drugs might have a negative repercussion down the line…It was very naive, but it was like an adult Disneyland, and my father kind of brought me into this world. It's a bit twisted, and I wouldn't do it with my kid, but I don't think he realized how profoundly deadly drug use could be…I don't blame people for my shortcomings and disasters. They're all mine…my dad and I were partners in crime…Without his influence, I'd be pushing pencils somewhere.

In a first-hand recollection of the routine debauchery that defined his home life, Kiedis recalled, "I was the only child present for all this insanity. For the most part, the adults who didn't know me just ignored me." Kiedis cited one of his father's best friends, Who drummer Keith Moon, as an exception to that rule. He described the legendarily rowdy drummer as someone who, in response to the craziness, "always tried to make me feel at ease…In the midst of this chaotic, riotous, party-life atmosphere where everyone was screaming and shouting and sniffing and snorting and drinking and humping, Moon would take me under his arm and say: 'How you doing, kid? Are you having a good time? Shouldn't you be in school or something? Well, I'm glad you're here, anyway.'"

Kiedis grew up throughout the 1970s on a rock 'n' roll pallet as that ranged from Sly and the Family Stone to Led Zeppelin and Parliament Funkadelic to Stevie Wonder, all of whom he would later credit with influencing his evolution as a musician. While attending Fairfax High School as a freshman, Anthony met his instant best friend and future band mate, Flea.

Michael 'Flea' Balzary was born on October 16th, 1962 in Melbourne, Australia, to biological father Mick Balzary and mother,

Patricia. He wouldn't land in Los Angeles until a decade later, following his parents' divorce and his mother's remarriage to stepfather Walter Urban Jr. A jazz bassist, Flea was raised on the same legends his stepfather idolized, including Louis Armstrong, Miles Davis, and Dizzy Gillespie—the latter of whom Flea especially admired. Based in large part on the influence of his aforementioned idols, Flea chose the trumpet as his first musical instrument. He displayed a near prodigy command of the instrument; it even landed him a brief gig with the Los Angeles Junior Philharmonic Orchestra. Flea recalled one of his childhood highlights. At age 12 after attending a Dizzy Gillespie concert with his mother he "snuck backstage, and there's Dizzy, holding his trumpet, talking to someone…I run up to him, and I'm like, 'Mr. Gillespie.' And I can't even talk. I'm in awe. And he just puts his arm around me and hugs me real tight, so my head's kind of in his armpit. He smiles and just holds me there for, like, five minutes while he talks. I'm just frozen in joy—oh my God, oh my God, oh my God."

Still, in spite of the joy he found in the musical environment of his youth, the bassist at the same time recalled that "I was raised in a very violent, alcoholic household…and had a very violent upbringing…I grew up being terrified of my parents, particularly my father figures…My stepfather was an aggressive alcoholic…and had shoot-outs with the cops. I slept in the backyard because I was scared. In a way, it gave me freedom." By the time Flea and Anthony Kiedis had partnered up as high school freshmen in the fall of 1977, Flea's troubled home-life and Anthony's freedom given his father's social schedule gave the two access to a very different high school experience. "Anthony and I were street kids, basically…by the time I was 12 or 13, I was out until three or four in the morning, carousing, on drugs. Elaborating on what made the pair click, Kiedis recalled that "we were drawn to each other by the forces of mischief and love and we became virtually inseparable. We were both social outcasts. We found each other and it turned out to be the longest lasting friendship of my life." The duo would soon immerse themselves in Hollywood, which, as Flea explained, they were both drawn to because "whether it be street kids from broken homes like me and Anthony, or victims of huge racism like the black community, or the Mexican community, crawling across the border just to survive. There are pockets where all these people come together and live in a creative and vibrant atmosphere, and that's the Los Angeles I love."

In addition to the usual juvenile escapades, Flea and Anthony also found themselves drawn together by a creative chemistry that grew out of their mutual musical affinity for the burgeoning punk movement that seized Hollywood in the late 1970s. Centering on the legendary Starwood Night Club, Kiedis recalled a social setting in which he and Flea "were hanging out in the parking lot, mostly… trying to sneak into Germs and Black Flag and Circle Jerks shows." Elaborating more on what drew the outlaw pair to punk, Flea explained that "the beautiful thing about punk rock was the intensity, the energy. And punk deflated the whole bloated rock-star thing. I think that musicians who don't pay attention to punk have a gap in their knowledge that makes it difficult to communicate in this day in age." In addition to punk, the pair had a healthy love for another budding new musical style: hip-hop. Kiedis had seen live shows by Grandmaster Flash and the Furious Five. To that end, Kiedis recalled the true weight of the rap group's impression on him as "mind-blowing…I subconsciously vowed I would somehow create that type of energy to entertain others. I didn't have a clue how to write a song or sing, but I thought I could probably figure out how to tell a story in rhythm."

While the best of friends, Kiedis and Flea wouldn't become band mates until well after Flea's first foray into the process as an impromptu member of Anthym, formed in 1979 during his junior year of high school. Formed with future RHCP members Hillel Slovak on guitar and Jack Irons on drums, the group was fronted on vocals and lead guitar by Alain Johannes. Flea quickly picked up bass, playing by ear to guitarist Hillel Slovak's lines. Soon thereafter, Anthym won second place in a local 'Battle of the Bands' contest, prompting them to begin gigging locally around Hollywood, with Kiedis as their resident number one fan, having already befriended Irons and Slovak as fellow Fairfax High School students. Anthym would soon change their name to What is This? They attracted such attention at local punk club gigs that Flea was asked to join legendary local punk outfit FEAR, signed at the time to Slash Records. Flea only stayed briefly with FEAR during 1982 before leaving to form his own group with Kiedis, who by this point had dropped out of UCLA to pursue music full time. As Kiedis recalled, "Flea, Hillel and I were friends way before we formed a band…We'd go to clubs together, go up to San Francisco and do drugs together."

The band was initially formed under the moniker Tony Flow and the Miraculously Magestic Masters of Mayhem. During a jam session that Kiedis described as "an art-funk installation piece," the singer recalled that the band's chemistry was "so electrifying we all thought, 'We have to do this again next week.'" The band played their first official live gig soon after at the Rhythm Lounge club, quickly becoming a house act. Making the decision to change band names as their crowds rapidly grew, the band soon settled on the Red Hot Chili Peppers, which Kiedis described as inspired by the notion of "American tradition, like Louis Armstrong and the Red Hot Five." In late 1983, the Chili Peppers entered Bijou Studios to record a 9-song demo that eventually landed them an 8-album record deal with E.M.I. Records.

Part II
The Red Hot Chili Peppers

1984

In the spring of 1984, the Red Hot Chili Peppers stepped into a recording studio under contract with E.M.I. Records to record their debut LP, *The Red Hot Chili Peppers*. The album was produced by Gang of Four's Andrew Gill and engineered by future Alternative Rock production God Dave Jerden (who would later make ground-breaking albums with Jane's Addiction and Alice in Chains). According to Anthony Kiedis, the band's first attempt to capture their already-legendary live blend of funk, punk, rap, and metal on analog tape at El Dorado Studios in L.A. was "inspired by people… like Parliament/ Funkadelic, Sly and the Family Stone, Run-D.M.C. and the Beastie Boys." Expanding on the latter, bassist Flea added that a number of other bands were also influential, including "Gang of Four, Defunkt, Grandmaster Flash. There were the Big Boys, Konk, and the Brainiacs. A lot of rock bands were drawing from funk and rap, but a lot of it was done in a very arty kind of way." Flea also emphasized punk rock's influence over the band by reasoning that "what punk rock was about to me was never having to say you are sorry…I love the Germs. They were one of the best bands ever."

According to the album's producer, Andrew Gill,

> prior to working with the Chili Peppers, I'd…produced an EP for Busta Jones. I'd always kind of produced a lot with Gang of Four…When I produced Red Hot Chili Peppers…I found it very straightforward, just really a contin-uation of what I'd be doing there. They were very up-front about being fans of Gang of Four. When they said would I come and produce their album, they told me 'We're totally

into Gang of Four. That's why we want you to come along.' Obviously, there's a very big connection there. That kind of guitar-orientated thing obviously owes a fair bit to Gang of Four...Flea and Anthony told me many times that the Gang of Four song 'Not Great Men' was the most central song for them getting into music and forming a band.

Bassist Flea described the impression Gang of Four's sound had made on him as a musician growing up: "it completely changed the way I looked at rock music and sent me on my trip as a bass player...At the time, we loved and looked up to Andy Gill so much, and those first couple of Gang of Four records he made definitely stand up as some of the great all-time rock records and definitely were a big influence on us."

Along with musical anchors Anthony Kiedis and Flea, the band's line-up for the album's recording included Jack Sherman on guitar and Captain Beefheart drummer Cliff Martinez hitting the skins. Flea explained, "we thought Andy would be perfect for us, because the Gang of Four albums were so fantastic...Their first two albums were hugely influential records...Gang of Four are one of the finest bands that England has ever produced, and, consciously or subconsciously, they have influenced a lot of things that we write. They had the English, white angst funk thing happening... That was our first record and our whole thing was being punk about the funk."

Still, in spite of the band's initial excitement over working with Gill on their debut LP, according to Flea, they quickly discovered that "it was a different point of view that we had going into things...our natural, spontaneous thing wasn't there. If we'd had the original line-up, I think...we would have gotten the real thing, hardcore, down on record. We were so explosive at that time and it's not an explosive record...we knew what we wanted... we wanted a raw fucking rock album."

Gill's desire to make a radio-friendly album disagreed so fundamentally with the band's desire to remain true to their funk-metal roots that Flea recalled he found "we wanted to go for a sound like the Gang of Four albums he had produced…not as sparse, but with the same raw funkness. But when we got together he wasn't into the same thing anymore. That's disheartening, because those are great records." Recalling some specific examples of musical miscommunication that defined the recording process, Anthony Kiedis explained that Gill "thought it was necessary to use rhythm machines as our drums because that was what was getting on the radio at the time. He took it that we had to do whatever it took to conform to the sound of the radio." Flea elaborated, "We weren't about to compromise our sound, which was based on organic bass and drums. It was a seriously different point of view that we had about going into things."

Flea joked later that Gil might have been "too English for us…He had a dry, holier-than-thou English way…so things didn't go as smoothly as we would have liked." Part of that latter inability, as engineer Dave Jerden recalled, rested squarely with the band's behavior in the course of venting their frustrations: "they'd be saying to Gill 'We hate you—fuck off and die!' They treated him poorly." Regardless, Jerden complimented the producer's bedside manner in maintaining a level head, explaining that Gill "was a total English gentleman. I'd be arguing with Kiedis and Flea, and he'd be oblivious to what was going on. He was totally together, he was amazing."

Years later, Gill demonstrated his skill for diplomacy in artist-producer relations: "Flea is the most vocal member of the band… Sometimes I read things where…he's said 'Andy Gill, he's a bastard and I hate that record.' Other times he says how he really wants to apologize to me…but that's just Flea; it's water off a duck's back to me."

In acknowledgement of the latter, Flea noted:

> I had no fucking idea what we were doing in a big fancy recording studio making a big fancy record… We should

have been asking 'Can't we try something?' but we didn't know. He was a very uptight Englishman on top of it, so that mix didn't work very well... We didn't have a groove at that time. We had Cliff and Jack and I don't think that configuration was capable of creating a powerful groove.

Years later, former guitarist Jack Sherman asked "why didn't they say 'Thank you or no thank you and move on? They didn't realize that they had any power; they didn't realize they had any choices. Was it because he was the only producer available? They were blowing it constantly. I thought they were clueless...Gill just recorded the sound of the day...There were good moments, they're just hard to remember."

Gill, for his part, reasoned that "they saw me as a hero in the beginning of this process and they didn't quite know what to expect in the studio...I've dealt with a lot of bands that were inexperienced and trying to get them to understand the recording process is really crucial. Sometimes you succeed better than others... They were completely green; they thought producers just hung around and stroked their egos. Then when I started saying 'You should do more of this and less of that,' they started going 'Hey.'"

The band's debut album fell short of capturing the band's core sound. Anthony Kiedis explained, "What we originally set out to do was to be complete and utter perpetrators of hardcore, bone-crushing mayhem... To try and describe that to another musician and have it mean something is nearly impossible." Kiedis wasn't speaking just of the band's producer but also of stand-in guitarist Jack Sherman, who Gill recalled "had problems with the band on a psychological kind of level. Flea and Anthony picked on him a lot."

Band leaders Anthony Kiedis and Flea pursued an electrified sound that they militantly enforced in the studio, going to the extreme, as producer Andy Gill recalled, with a track called 'True Men' featuring acoustic guitar: "halfway through the take the door opening with... Anthony screaming 'What's that sound?' When I said it was an acoustic guitar, he said 'That's fucking homo!', grabbed the guitar off Jack, threw it to the ground, and said 'No fucking homo acoustic guitar on my record.'" To solve the problem, Gill and Sherman resorted to what the guitarist recalled as "guerilla recording, because they were so destructive, blowing it constantly…Most of the good guitar playing was done while Anthony and Flea weren't there… Anything that was the 'Little Wing' side of Hendrix was homo. I was almost beaten to death for that. I was frustrated—why couldn't we have a few chord changes? If it was pretty, it was not allowed."

Former drummer Cliff Martinez recalled a similar experience, citing an album throwaway track called 'Human Satellite,' which the drummer recalled, "terrified all of us. It was a commercial version of ourselves that we didn't like. Everybody in the band despised it." Flea further explained that "we wanted hard-edged funk…and Andy wanted namby-pamby pop-funk…we ended up with a record in between… To this day…I really regret our inability to deal with Andy."

Gill cited what he believed to be the principle obstacle in making headway with the band: "one of the main things that was perhaps a little contentious between us was what was the best material. To me, there was no doubt that the kind of super-fast surf-punk two-minute song style was all very well, but to me it seemed kind of boring…I said to them, this thing here, this thing you're doing, this is what I love and this is what is going to mark you out from the crowd. If you rely on this super-fast surf-punk thing, you're going to be just another west coast band with apparently dodgy politics."

Engineer Dave Jerden recalled that producer Gill "wanted to do more of a dance record, whereas people were into the Chili Peppers because they made a noise, and they were wild—Flea was like an animal, as was Anthony…It was one of the most God-awful experiences of my life…Gill and the band were fire and ice." Former drummer Cliff Martinez concluded that "Andy was in a different head space; he really wanted to make a commercial record." Regardless of their disagreements, eventually Gill and the Chili Peppers finished the album, which—in the producer's opinion—was "what they absolutely became known for…The funkier kind of stuff did eventually get featured a lot more than what they were originally wanting…The style and the songs that are most heavily featured on the A-side of that record went on to be more heavily developed with their second and third records. It was a route map, a blueprint, for the rest of their careers."

Years later, Flea diplomatically concluded that "I used to really regret that we didn't make the record I thought we could have, that it could have been a classic record. But Anthony recently pointed out to me that it was all part of our learning process and had we been too good, too fast we never would have continued the long and rich growing process we are still on…Our natural spontaneous thing wasn't there…If we'd had that original lineup—Jack Irons and Hillel Slovak instead of Jack Sherman and Cliff Martinez—on the first record, I think we would have been a lot more popular a lot sooner. We would have gotten the real thing, hard-core, down on record. We were so explosive at that time—and it's not an explosive record…still, the record has some great moments."

Part III
Freaky Styley

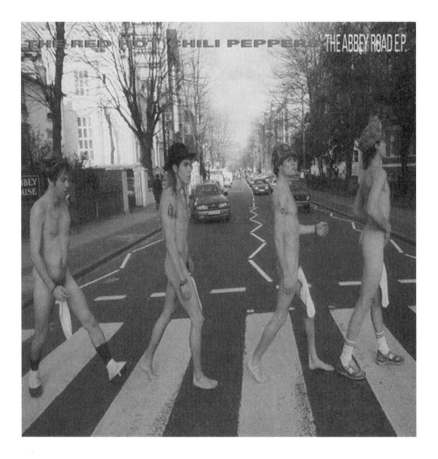

1985

While the Red Hot Chili Peppers' debut LP tanked commercially, it was instrumental in focusing and shaping the band's final sound, which from day one had a clear root in the Funk style Parliament Funkadelic mastermind George Clinton had founded a decade earlier. With their collaboration with Andy Gill solidly over, the band was in a fluid state musically, searching for a new producer and guitarist following a tour in late 1984. By February 1985, the band had ushered out guitarist Jack Sherman and eagerly re-embraced original axe man Hillel Slovak, who—fresh off the commercial failure of his other project, 'What is This'—returned to his rightful place alongside Anthony and Flea.

According to then-drummer Cliff Martinez, "things moved more smoothly with Hillel in the band. He was able to live and breathe and create...unlike Jack...Hillel was an open-minded guy...and could be both a cerebral player and a bit Neanderthal." Engineer Dave Jerden observed that Slovak "was real quiet, a real sweet kid. And he had this thing with his playing that to me was just like Hendrix—you don't learn it, it just comes naturally. It's a real cool, liquid type of playing." Jack Irons reflected, "I knew in my head that it was inevitable Hillel would go off with the Chilis...He enjoyed that funk kind of thing." Given the direction in which the band's sound was evolving via their collaboration with George Clinton, the addition of Slovak seemed both timely and logical.

Before heading into preproduction for the album, Flea flew to Detroit to meet Clinton, who he had hailed as "the epic mythological prolific genius himself, Dr Funkenstein." Elaborating on the meeting, the bassist recalled, "I was mighty nervous to meet him, but no one ever made me feel more comfortable more quickly—ever…I walked into his motel room and there he was, just the warmest, kindest, most beautiful person I've ever met in my life. That moment I will never forget…George is a beautiful person. He's a very warm man, good to be around. He's very inspirational; he's like an exploding cosmic love bomb that explodes in all directions."

Legendary Parliament bassist Bootsie Collins explained, "Flea will tell anyone who asks in a minute…Parliament-Funkadelic was one of his major influences. And now all the kids that dig the Peppers connect the musical dots and, the next thing you know, they're picking up a P-Funk record and going, 'Whoa!' To me, it's evolution. The new fans are going to keep taking it to the next level. Kids will say, 'I got into this because the Chili Peppers were doing it' and so on. It's all connected, whether the kids realize it or not."

The similarity between the Chili Peppers' stylistically-chameleon sound and Clinton's changing music made the bands' collaboration natural. The bassist reasoned that "they just did music they wanted to do and it didn't fit into any category…I think what we were doing is very similar, except that they came out of this acid/hippy thing and we came out of the punk-rock thing." Elaborating on the band's praise for and excitement at the prospect of working with Clinton, singer Anthony Kiedis termed the producer as "amazing…He's the ultimate hard-core funk creator in the world…Their music is so great, I don't think people are even capable of understanding how great it is…James Brown is the king of his field, but he was more pure funk. If anybody ever wanted to ask you what was the greatest funk/metal ever, it would be Parliament/Funkadelic."

With their respect for Clinton firmly intact, the band seemed eager for and open to direction from their idol. Flea explained, "one thing George Clinton told me about playing funk I'll never forget is 'You have to take it all the way home.'" Elaborating on the latter, Anthony Kiedis explained, "He's just a bottomless pit of funky creativity who I have a great deal of respect for." Underscoring just how high up his respect for Clinton's opinion and tutelage sat, Flea recalled one moment during recording where the producer had interrupted him mid-track with a suggestion, something that had Andy Gill done: "I'd be screaming 'Shut the fuck up! I'm trying to play!' But George could get away with it." Prior to beginning principle tracking, the band had begun preproduction at Clinton's farm just outside Detroit, and later at an in-town studio Detroit On Parade. Drummer Cliff Martinez fondly recalled the preproduction sessions as "a kick. We had our instruments set up in George's living room. Every day we'd wander out in our bathrobes and play and George would talk about arrangements."

Moving into United Sound Recording Studios in Detroit proper to begin tracking for *Freaky Styley*, sessions typically began in the early evening—Clinton's preference—and went until morning. Clinton's style of producing stood in stark contrast to that of Andy Gill, such that, as Flea recalled, the band had no problem taking direction from Clinton: Clinton's voice "was the greatest sounding thing I ever heard. We'd be out there rocking and his voice would come in, 'Yeeeah git it…Come on now! Dig deep!' And so forth." Anthony Kiedis, in recalling some of his favorite moments being produced by Clinton, explained that "what he does with vocal arranging is incredible and the experience we had working with him I wouldn't trade for a penthouse suite in the Empire State Building. I'm so fortunate to have had that experience of making a record with him. It was a blessing to be able to hang out with him and learn from him and be part of his whole feeling there."

Drummer Cliff Martinez, for his part, explained that, in contrast to the tense creative atmosphere that had defined the band's debut LP, during the *Freaky* sessions the band "had fun in the studio. George told us not to be intimidated. There was a controlled party atmosphere in the studio, with people sitting around, ready to do handclaps. I remember smoking a pile of pot and—this is awful to say but I discovered that drugs could be a tool. I played much better, with that particular type of music, when I was stoned. I felt I played so much better than on the first record, in part because of this loose, party-type atmosphere."

In addition to the four principle band members, the extended musical family for the *Freaky* sessions included a trio of horn players dubbed the 'Horny Horns' composed of Fred Wesley, Maceo Parker, and Benny Cowan, as well as percussionist Larry Fratangelo and backing vocalists Andre Williams, Steve Boyd, Gary Shider, and Michael 'Clip' Payne. Among the most personally historic moments was when Clinton himself joined the bassist on the background vocals for 'If You Want Me To Stay.' Flea reflected, "I was in fucking heaven…Me in the same room with the great mythological hero Dr. Funkenstein, him singing…with our band." Upon completion of principle tracking, Flea exuded a contagious satisfaction with the results, explaining that "I feel great about this record, about the way we played. After we just didn't get the groove of who we were all the way through the first record, I was so happy just to hear deep groove come out of the speakers when we were recording this music."

Many critics, as well as the band, have credited Clinton with being the first producer to truly put the Red Hot Chili Peppers in touch with their funk-metal roots. George Clinton's manager Archie Ivy recalled of the result the pair achieved: "they said they wanted to be funky… George really taught them how to be funky. They lived for a time with George. He said, 'Look boys, you got the funk, but because you're white, you're gonna make it to the top before we do." Indeed, *Freaky Styley* would mark the band's debut on the industry's radar.

Rolling Stone was among the first mainstream giants to recognize the band as "irreverent, punky rockers with a jones for rhythm and blues vernacular, both lyrical and musical, and a commitment to humor, variety, and unbridled stylistic independence." At the same time, *Interview Magazine* deemed the band to be "the absolute funk-rock Matrix." Meanwhile, the musical credibility the band had gained with the rock press via their collaboration with Clinton seemed enough to secure their place, as what *All Music Guide* concluded was the "accessible successors of P-Funk."

The band's stylistic blend of rap, metal, and funk gained them enough credibility to land an opening slot on Run DMC's 1986 'Raising Hell' tour. The band's rock audience was also rapidly expanding to include the suburban skateboarding demographic, who were drawn to the foot the Chili Peppers still had firmly planted in punk and thrash rock. As far as the comparisons people drew between the Chilis and the Beastie Boys—both considered the pioneers of rap-rock, lead singer Anthony Kiedis didn't fight them, reasoning that "the Beastie Boys are white, they rap. I'm white, I rap. By them having success, it makes it more plausible for us."

Still, bassist Flea felt the band's chances at success at the time were penalized by the fact that "the album was too funky for white radio, and too punk rockin' for black radio." When they weren't supporting Run DMC, the band kept in touch with the core audience of punk and skate rockers who populated their shows by the. It was here that the band's live shows became the stuff of legend, spawning a following that grew via a grass-roots, word-of-mouth about everything from the band's habit of playing shows wearing only socks over their privates to crowd-surfing riots, arrests, and massive drug use on the part of band members.

Another line-up change brought Jack Irons back on drums by March 1986, rounding out the band's original line-up in a move bassist Flea explained as happening because "Hillel was ready to come back to the fold…Cliff thought we were heading in too conventional a rock type of sound so Jackie came back to his brethren." With Jack Irons back on drums, the band had an opportunity during their endless touring to solidify as a foursome, which to newly seated drummer Irons made sense as "we had a lot of work to do because the Red Hot Chili Peppers hadn't put out a record since 1985 and the next one wasn't coming until 1987."

Part IV
The Uplift Mofo Party Plan

1987

According to MTV.com, 1987's *The Uplift Mojo Party Plan* was the Red Hot Chili Peppers' first "album...to make an impression." The third studio LP in the band's short 4-year recording career, it would sadly be their last with guitarist Hillel Slovak, who would die a year later just as the band was beginning to live up to their full potential musically. Ironically, while *The Uplift Mofo Party Plan* was the band's most focused LP in context of what would become their trade-mark musical stylings, Flea would later describe the time surrounding the writing and recording of the LP as "a gloomy time in our career...Drug use was really beginning to make a morose stand." Putting the aforementioned bleakness in context of its extremity, eventual resident producer Rick Rubin—who first met with the group in 1987—felt the band was at too low a point personally to excel.

As Rubin recalled, the gray skies hanging over the band at the time, "it was a very unhealthy...depressed feeling in the room... Just bad news, negativity all around, lack of organization between band members...and a lack of trust...It was kind of the height of the unhealthy version of the original line-up...I remember going to a rehearsal...and musically it felt good, but the energy in the room felt dangerous." Echoing Rubin's sentiment, bassist Flea explained that upon their first meeting, "we did not connect with Rick. That vibe was very weird...Our communication was not healthy."

Chaotic by their very nature, the band's focus came from producer Michael Beinhorn, who quipped he took the gig because "at that particular point, no one else wanted to work with them." Hailed routinely by *Rolling Stone* over the years for his "sure hand" and "slamming production." Beinhorn's goals for the album revolved at their most basic around "trying to make a record that would help them survive at that point… They were reviled by their record company…there were certain people that would have been happy to see them languish into invisibility…It's difficult to say…whether or not the band was prepared to make an album… It was, however, essential to their survival at that point."

Elaborating on his reasons for taking on a band and album nobody else wanted to produce, Beinhorn explained, "I felt I could probably make a record with just about anyone, and I wanted to work with them, so it was a combination of elements really." In contrast with the recording of *Freaky Styley*, Beinhorn would set a different tone. Bassist Flea explained, "working with George Clinton, we spent a lot of time partying. He works by creating a real jovial atmosphere to record in. Working with Michael Beinhorn, it was done very efficiently. We worked. Sure, we joked around, but we also spent a lot of time in the studio making it happen…He was a professional type of producer guy." Putting even a finer point on the contrast between Clinton and Beinhorn, singer Anthony Kiedis recalled that Beinhorn was "very anal-retentive."

The latter discipline was appropriate given the circumstances the producer and band were working under. According to Beinhorn, in addition to the band's drug habit, there was "a very small amount of money to work with." Perhaps in an effort to spend their money wisely and give the band as much structural direction as, Beinhorn explained, "everything…on the record was created while we were in preproduction. It took a lot of work and a lot of concentration… They didn't use many structural elements…This was not much different than other creative situations I'd been in. As for being prepared, that was never a strong suit for the band. Then again, they worked up most of the structures in rehearsal."

Beinhorn wanted to "build off their first 2 albums, I knew I could use the inconsistencies in songwriting and performance to underscore and illuminate what if felt the band needed and help get them to the next level. I felt that in some ways they were in a creative rut and I wanted to do what I could to get them out of it."

Still, in spite of the aforementioned improvements, Beinhorn sought to adhere strictly to the band's foundational musical elements, explaining that he "didn't want to really compromise for the sake of the artist." Recording got underway in May of 1987 at Capitol Studios Studio B, with a budget of $120,000.00. Beinhorn described a workday routine that began near sun down, reasoning that "I think most people who have a recording artist's type of job tend to be more oriented toward the evening, and the Chili Peppers were no different." Describing his experiences working individually with band members once proper recording had begun, Beinhorn recalled that Flea "was there to work. He didn't do a lot of fucking about when it came to recording. He was pretty serious and put his all into whatever he did."

Where recording lead singer Anthony Kiedis was concerned, Beinhorn encountered more of a challenge due to the vocalist's drug habit, which the producer explained complicated recording periodically so that "it was impossible to get any contribution from him whatsoever…When we had demos with full instrumental tracks, and Anthony had to come up with lyrics and melodies, he would instead show up with lyrics for a song the band had cut a while before and shelved, as it was mediocre. It was infuriating to everyone, and I got so angry with him that I threw him out…We would lose Anthony for weeks at a time while he'd stay at his girlfriend's house and shoot up." By contrast, Beinhorn explained that when Kiedis was sober and focused in the studio, "he worked really hard. I think he knew that he was up against a lot, and when he was challenged, he really rose to the occasion and did his best. He was definitely another stylist. When you hear his voice, you know it's him. There's no question about it."

As far as the album's guitar tracks were concerned, Beinhorn recalled that guitarist Hillel Slovak had "a very unusual approach to the whole thing. It was Hendrixy, and definitely influenced by a lot of James Brown stuff, but still a whole other thing. He was a stylist as well. I would never characterize him as a songwriter; he was more of a parts writer. Recording Hillel, he had his days. Some days he was more on, other days he was more in the clouds. But he could definitely play, no question about it." Detailing his technical set-up in recording the band, Beinhorn recalled that "we recorded on a Neve console, and we didn't track any of the records live. At that point in time, it had to do with wanting to get a certain sound and separation, but I was finding that a lot of bands who were great live bands didn't play well together in the studio. In the case of the Chilis, tracking live didn't work out, so we had to track everything separately."

Beginning with the album's drum sound, whose micing scheme the producer categorized as "fairly rudimentary," Beinhorn attributes the overall effect of the album to then drummer Jack Irons, reasoning that "like in most cases where people say 'Oh, that drum sound was amazing,' you also have to remember first that you have to start with an amazing drummer. And with those guys, if they've had one thing, they've always had the best drummers. Jack Irons was one of my favorite drummers of all time; he was just a remarkable drummer. I think a lot of the drum sound we got had to do with his playing. I would go so far as to say it's not easy to make Jack sound bad. He knows how to hit."

Beinhorn elaborated further on tracking Irons: "we wound up working with an orange Ludwig kit, which we didn't have a budget to even rent drums, so we just took the best that we had." Once drum tracks had been laid, Beinhorn brought in Flea to track bass lines, and described a productive climate where "when we were tracking, he was quite technically proficient. He recorded DI—direct input—there was no amp." Beinhorn further reflected, "he's a great musician, and is extremely talented. His sense of timing and feel is really, really good. Harmonically, for a bass player, I always found him to be a cut above, as well. He's a very rhythmic bass player, and I think his choice of root notes is always very, very good. He's a stylist, and definitely one of a kind."

Flea, for his part, placed a heavy emphasis in his playing on funk, reasoning that "today's funk isn't very funky to me…It's just too clean. Funk should be dirty music; it's not pristine, it's gotta have that dirty grungy feel." Where tracking Hillel Slovak was concerned, Beinhorn recalled that "he played through Marshalls," and further explained that the guitarist was a professional who by and large controlled his drug habit such that "he would never let it interfere with his work until *Uplift* was completed."

Once backing tracks had been successfully laid and Beinhorn's attention turned to recording Anthony Kiedis' lead vocals, the producer detailed an involved process, where, due to the large presence of singing on the album, "he definitely had a hard time hitting pitch on a lot of stuff, and we didn't have pitch correction back then, so the way we would do it is: if we had a melody line, I would go and sing the melody part, and then go and double-track just to re-enforce it. Then when he was in the booth singing, I would go in and kind of sing it to his ear while he was in there singing as well. So it was definitely a process. We cut vocals at a variety of different studios." Beinhorn fondly recalled, "at one point, I remember I tried experimenting with a double-mic array where we used an Eli 251 together with a AKG P-48 414 on a song called 'Love Trilogy.'"

Aside from the aforementioned experimentation, Beinhorn explained, "I don't recall there being a lot of effects on that record." The band was elated with the recorded album once the principle tracking was completed. Singer Anthony Kiedis qualified the latter by recalling that the finished album put the band "into a state of inspired excitement. We were all very tickled by how good our record was sounding. I was especially blessed because a few months earlier I had been kicked out of the band for being too wrapped up in drug addiction to rock out. This was now a time of celebration and elation." Even Beinhorn signaled his clear sense of accomplishment upon completion of the album's tracking, fondly joking that after all the challenges in the course of recording, "I had developed a certain amount of affection for these guys."

Flea summarized the album's recording process: "there were mishaps and nearly breaking up…but also some good inspiring moments… We were crazy as shit and on a highway to hell, but we did it, we pulled it off and we made a record we are proud of…It wasn't all bad, we did have a lot of fun, too." In amplifying the latter and perhaps best summing up where the band was at the time—musically and personally—guitarist Hillel Slovak, commented, "I'm high on coke—too many drugs… but I really enjoyed it for the album sessions…It was fun…I'm so extremely proud of everybody's work—it is at times genius. Anthony's words are really something else. This is going to be a hit—it has to be—every track is sooo good."

The bassist further elaborated on his feelings of the band's accomplishments: "as far as that record goes, I think it's the most complete record that we've ever made, and I'm happy with every aspect of it. I think it's captured the live intensity of the band and it's captured different aspects of what we play musically…Uplift is probably the rockingest record we ever made. I don't mean the best, though to some it might be, I just mean in terms of straight up rockin' and not giving a fuck—making some art. This record really brings the rock, funk, and art in just the way we wanted to at the time…Overall, it was a strange time in our career, but I really see it as being a rock solid booming and interesting record… When the Peppers formed…we had a very important secret plan. First was to make a great record. Second step was to make a great video. And the third step was to make a great tour. We figure we've done step one with *The Uplift Mojo Party Plan*. As far as that record goes, I think it's captured the live intensity of the band and it's captured different aspects of what we play musically."

Part V
Mother's Milk

1989

T*he Uplift Mofo Party Plan* put the Red Hot Chili Peppers on the commercial map for the first time, debuting at #134 on the Billboard Top 200 Album Chart—the band's first showing ever. Any celebration was ultimately eclipsed by the tragic passing of guitarist Hillel Slovak from a lethal heroin overdose in September 1988. In the tragedy's aftermath, the band coped via the time-honored tradition: they used the creative process of rock 'n' roll as therapy to overcome their sadness—to what degree they could. Out of the process, the band would produce their most sophisticated and commercially accessible album up to that point.

Elaborating on the latter in action, singer Anthony Kiedis explained, "we tried to use our loss as a bolstering, positive experience…We knew that we weren't done yet…That the life of the Red Hot Chili Peppers still had untapped creative energy that we didn't want to go to waste and that Flea and I were still best friends…Hillel is responsible for the sound we created…Losing your best friend at age 26 is a mind- and soul-blower. But there was definitely an inspiration that came from Hillel dying, which helped sharpen the focus of the band."

Years later, Kiedis, in reflecting on the Chili Peppers' decision to go forward, further underscored the transitional importance of *Mother's Milk* on a broader level: the band not only had to get past Slovak's passing, but also out of the shadows in to realize their full commercial potential. Kiedis explained, "it's so beautiful to think about our spirit back then, doing that album, and I get these mini little retrospectives of our life, in a real beautiful way…It's great… that feeling, because it was really the end of an era…for us…when we recorded that album. That was the transition when we went from being a pretty underground band, playing little theaters and stuff and sleeping on people's floors, doing whatever we did to get by, to becoming a mainstream band."

Using their life-long friendship and musical kinship as a foundation, Kiedis and Flea went about re-inventing the band's line-up. The band's creative fire was also re-ignited by the injection of a new drummer, Chad Smith. Producer Michael Beinhorn detailed the seemingly endless search the band endeavored on in finding Smith— who joined the band two weeks prior to their entering the studio:

> it was funny because, when they were doing drummer auditions, Chad was the second- or third-to-last drummer they saw, and the second he came in and started playing, I said 'Pick this guy, pick this guy.' And at first, they didn't like him because he basically looked like he should have been in Poison or something. He had a bandana on and his hair was kind of funny, and they were like 'He doesn't fit the image at all.' And I was like 'Just listen to this fucking guy play! Just pick him.' And they waited days, and I was like 'You guys have to be kidding me, this fucking guy is perfect! He's the man! Pick him.' So finally they were like 'Oh, alright' and picked him.

Anthony Kiedis recalled,

> all the drummers who auditioned were basically weako-potamuses. They just didn't have the emotional intensity or the physical talent to rock the Peppers…Chad was like a human Roman candle, spiraling out these intense musical spasms… I remember thinking 'I don't know if this guy understands the funk, but that could come in time…But he is amazing. His drumming just hits that part of my brain…This monster walks in from Detroit, sits down behind the drums. Explodes on contact. It left us in a state of frenzied laughter that we couldn't shake ourselves out of

for half an hour. We hired the guy…He was a human power plant behind the drums.

Flea summed up Smith's audition by explaining that "all of a sudden…we thought 'This guy is playing his ass off,' and everything else went by the wayside…Chad sat down and lit a fire under our asses…It was an intense jam."

With Smith on board, as *Rolling Stone* would report in their coverage of the group, the band's fortunes got even "better when the band…recruited fan boy-guitar-wunderkind John Frusciante as Slovak's replacement." An extraordinarily emotional and challenging process of elimination, the band settled on the 19-year-old musical prodigy and multi-instrumentalist as their lead guitarist after being introduced by the Dead Kennedys' drummer D.H. Peligro. Frusciante, a religious fan of the band, described his reaction: when "Flea and Anthony called me… I kept real cool, but then I put the phone down and ran across the house and jumped up on the wall, there was these foot marks on the wall of the apartment…their music meant everything to me…I thought it was the most perfect, beautiful music that I had heard in my life. The wide variety of emotions in the music inspired me. Just the whole attitude of the band and the way they thought, and the way they looked, and—just everything. I felt it was a direct extension of my own personality…I really felt like part of the band."

In terms of reactions from Frusciante's new community of fellow band members, Flea, who had first jammed with the guitarist prior to his formal audition, felt the guitarist was "really talented and knowledgeable musically. He knows all the shit I don't know. I basically know nothing about music theory, and he's studied it to death, inside out. He's a very disciplined musician—all he cares about is his guitar and his cigarettes." Speaking in a broader musical context, producer Michael Beinhorn felt "it was apparent early on that John was the perfect guitarist for the band—he brought the elements of songwriting and composition to the band which they'd never truly had prior to his involvement. I believe that John is a pivotal figure in the Chili Peppers, being that he is such a distinctive songwriter."

Arguably, with the induction of new guitarist—John Frusciante— the band added the most important missing piece to rounding out the multi-colored pallet that would define the band's sound melodically and structurally in the years to come. This was especially true in the aforementioned context of songwriting. Frusciante explained how he felt that the band's creative process evolved:

> the songs that we write are really weird. They're not like anybody else. Most people write songs, and they have chord progressions, and maybe a riff, and so on. But ours…These multiple colors that each person sets up on their instrument, and they're totally independent of each other. The guitar part and the bass part only relate to each other in the sense of feeling, but they don't do the same thing. They weave in and out of each other. I always feel like Flea's sense of rhythm comes out of the fact that he started out on trumpet, and that jazz was the music that made him want to be a musician. But while he's never consciously tried to apply that knowledge to the bass, on bass he's only tried to play funk and punk rock and so on, it is still in his spiritual make-up. The types of rhythms and melodies he plays on bass—the only person who has sounded as rooted in jazz as Flea, that appealed to a rock audience has been Jack Bruce, who is my favorite bass player.

Ironically, in spite of the Chili Peppers' funk, Frusciante explained that "I wasn't really a funk player before I joined the band…I learned everything I needed to know about how to sound good with Flea by studying Hillel's playing, and I just took it sideways from there."

Elaborating on the band's songwriting process with Frusciante for *Mother's Milk*, the guitarist described a creative democracy where everybody is their own boss. I write the guitar parts, Chad does the drums and Flea writes the bass and Anthony writes the vocals. Everybody makes suggestions about everybody else's part. If you really want to do that part, you can do it, but everybody takes suggestions from everybody else...When we write songs, it's like building a house. Chad for instance, might decide on the perimeters, you know, how big the house is going to be, and what area of space the floor is going to cover. And then another person puts the walls on it, and then another person puts the roof and the ceiling on it, and then another person makes it look a certain way inside. And that's how our songs are put together, with each person doing their bit to create the final thing. We jam a lot and improvise, which is some thing that sets us apart from a lot of other bands, I think, particularly if their styles don't lend themselves to jamming. We improvise, and we're really good at it.

The guitarist continued,

every time we rehearse, we record at least five different jams that could make great songs. It's usually just us that just jam and jam and jam, and then Anthony starts dancing round to one of the jams and tells us that that's got to be a song, and then we think about what the next section should be like. Writing songs comes very naturally. It's not hard at all. Like I said, we just jam and the songs come out of it. We actually come up with way more material than we would need to come up with for an album. So then we generally just leave it up to Anthony to tell us which pieces of music he feels should be taken further into finished song form.

Expanding on his individual writing method, Frusciante explained that "a song is something spirits can get feelings from, but it's nothing a human being can be aware of—except I am. So they give it to me as just a color and as a vibe and as a feeling and as an aesthetic echo in my head, and then I'm able to take it and turn it into music."

Developing material and as a band in the same time, the Chili Peppers' writing routine, according to Frusciante, blossomed "mostly from jams. One guy will have an idea that he came up with, and show up at the studio; say it's a really cool bass line, and I'll make up a guitar part. I might have a guitar part that would make a good bridge or a good chorus. Sometimes we'll work together on something. Other times we'll just be jamming and come across a groove that sounds real good, and we'll try to make that into a song. Then we'll throw it away and write a new song."

Anthony Kiedis felt that Frusciante added his own creativity, in the compositional context. According to Kiedis, Frusciante brought "more melodic potential, so we explored that avenue and came up with songs like 'Knock Me Down.' That was something we didn't previously do, because it wasn't part of the talent in the band as it was before." Expanding even further, Flea added that the guitarist introduced "a new, melodic, chord-change-based style of songwriting to our band that wasn't there before…Most of the previous songs were groove based and had started with bass lines…It was an immense new element to the sound of our band and a big opening up for us."

Detailing the latter change more specifically, Flea explained,

> a lot of our funk songs start with the bass line. Some haven't. I love to play the funk bass. I live for it. It's what I do. The rhythm and the feel is what makes the funk. The bass is an integral part of that. On this album, there are some songs where the bass was the inspiration: 'Good Time Boys,' 'Nobody Weird Like Me,' and 'Sexy Mexican Maid' started with bass but became a lot more. Most of the time, the songs are really a group effort. It's hard for me to categorize the songs. To me it's all Red Hot Chili Peppers. But everything we play is just my natural feel. It's not about

sitting down and trying to go for this or that feel. It's just about picking it up and playing until something feels good to be a song. It's not conscious or intellectual. It's very primal. Sometimes it's hard and fast, sometimes it's weird and psychedelic and sometimes it's slinky and funky. I just love to play.

Frusciante echoed and amplified the latter with illustration of his own: "just looking at the expression on Chad's face and seeing the way he plays a drum fill can make me play a certain way." Directly contracting their recording method for *The Uplift Mofo Party Plan*, Beinhorn and the band made a decision to track basic tracks live off the floor on *Mother's Milk*.

Bassist Flea elaborated that, aside from tightening the band as players, the revised recording method also informed the band's creative process:

We like to record as much live as possible…That was a time of a lot of very physical playing. We played hard and fast more than at any other time in our career, I think. A lot of chops were going down…We played constantly, got to know each other, and came up with the record…By the end of recording, we had no problem sitting there and grooving through that whole song live. We'd all be in the same room. Our amps would be somewhere else. That's the only way to get the interplay. If we all record separately and every part is perfect, it can never be as good as each one playing together, and each person hearing little nuances that can happen at the moment.

Guitarist John Frusciante felt recording any other way would have been to the band's detriment, arguing that "recording at separate times is more clinical and playing with other people is divine inspiration." There were exceptions to this approach. Frusciante's guitar and Anthony Kiedis' vocals were tracked separately. Flea explained, "the only place we did live vocals was with 'Fire,' which we did with the old band. We didn't do it on the last album because on a lot of the stuff, the vocals weren't done yet. But on the first and second album, and a lot of the third album, we did everything live. We didn't necessarily keep everything, but Anthony sang a scratch vocal while we played. The more live you can get it, the better. The more prepared you are, the more opportunity you have to play it live. The more cool you are, the better you'll pull it off."

Still, while the band sounded as though they had a much more enjoyable time recording their debut LP with Frusciante, producer Michael Beinhorn kept an all-business vibe in the studio. The producer reasoned that multiple takes of each track were necessary because "the Peppers are great players…as with all people, some of their takes were better than others and occasionally it was necessary to keep trying something until it was right." With high hopes for a commercial break-out for the band, the producer employed a disciplined recording regiment that, as guitarist John Frusciante explained, meant "in the studio…it was much more concentrated."

Recorded primarily at Ocean Way Studios in L.A. in the summer of 1989, Beinhorn recalled, "we went to the B room, the one that has the passive console with the APIs racked up on the wall." Amid the plethora of changes the band was experiencing at the time, they found themselves recording in a climate which boasted a much more supportive corporate backing than their last LP, as was reflected by the band's improved $178,000.00 recording budget. Nevertheless, Frusciante explained that from the band's perspective "on *Mothers Milk,* Michael Beinhorn had really pushed us. He had me quadrupling guitars…In some instances we simultaneously put five distorted guitar tracks and a piercing solo on top of the bass." Meanwhile, singer Anthony Kiedis categorized Beinhorn's production style as "heavy handed." Beinhorn, for his part, had correctly warned the band heading into recording not to "think you're in here simply to make a record…You're in here to fight a war."

Beinhorn paid particular attention to John Frusciante, reasoning that "recording *Mother's Milk* was his maiden voyage with the band, and he was just a little kid at that point, and this was his dream thing to do in the world basically. The Chili Peppers had been his favorite band since he was a little kid, and all of a sudden here he is playing with them. So that was a great big deal for him."

In channeling the guitarist's excitement into his playing, Beinhorn also capitalized on Frusciante's technical musical knowledge, explaining that he "had a grasp of the technique of music. I think he could actually read, unlike 90% of the guys who are in rock bands. He had a good grasp of music theory, and he just came at it from a completely different standpoint. Aside from being a really good guitarist, he had a pretty good sense of musical structure, which was unusual to the band. I think that was the turning point for the band having those kind of structural elements introduced into what they did, which they'd never ever even come close to before."

In contrasting the process of recording Frusciante with his previous experience doing so with Slovak, Beinhorn acknowledged that "it was definitely quite a contrast between him and Hillel… One thing I recall about working with the Chili Peppers when they had Hillel was they were more of a band that jammed ideas and were able to turn them into songs, whereas with John, he actually brought finished pieces to the table and the band would work them out. At least that was my experience working with them."

There was a change in the technical set-up needed for Frusciante. Beinhorn explained that at first "he came in with these Ibanez guitars, which had these Floyd Rose tremela systems on them and whatnot, which is completely antithetical to the whole vibe of the Chili Peppers. So they were very, very opposed to that whole thing, which was actually very funny. It took a little while but eventually John agreed not to use the Ibanez guitars. We hooked him up with a Strat and a Les Paul, which is more their kind of sound. I think he gravitated to Fenders after that. When recording John, I think we used 57s and 421s to mic him."

Frusciante added "back when we were recording *Mother's Milk*… our producer Michael Beinhorn pushed me into this metal-funk department, and I therefore played mainly hard riffs on the lower E-string." Addressing his process for tracking Flea's bass, Beinhorn recalled, "Flea by that album had a Mesa 400 bass rig. On that album, again, I think Flea showed how good a musician he is, and how talented a creative individual he is by being able to adapt to a completely different element. John bringing the structural element in is something that involved more harmonic and melodic complexity, which gave Flea the opportunity to go in a different direction…I remember one song that he'd actually written the bass line for that was a very fast 6/8 song, and required 16th notes all the way through. It was pretty fast, so he could really only get through a couple bars at a time, so there was a lot of punching in, and he was sweating and cursing up a storm. But what he was doing at that point, considering how he was playing using that Larry Graham style, it was close to impossible anyway."

With a new guitarist and drummer, the producer was re-inventing his recording routine just as the band was musically reinventing the way they played and recorded together. In contrasting Chad Smith with former drummer Jack Irons, Beinhorn noted, "Chad and Jack are two completely different drummers. Chad is fun to watch, because he's a real rock guy. Stylistically, they are different type players. Jack always seemed a little more controlled in the studio, and Chad always seemed a little nuttier and like a wild man, which didn't make him harder to record at all. He's technically very adept. Recording Chad, our mic set-up for his drums was a 57 on the top, 421s on the toms, 414s for overheads."

Where his attention turned to Anthony Kiedis' vocals, Beinhorn utilized the recording of one of the album's hit singles to illustrate a larger point. Because of the structural components Frusciante had introduced to the band's songwriting, "Anthony HAD to sing more on that record, because John came in with this song 'Knock Me Down,' and it had was the first song that the Chili Peppers did that had a real melodic flow to it. It wasn't these pentatonic, blues-based, scaley type things, or that was just shouted. They all liked the song, but when Anthony was recording his vocals, in general, I don't remember that he liked having a lot of people around when we were working, maybe because he was singing more."

Kiedis, for his part, explained that he was inspired by musical influences including "Bob Marley, John Lennon, and Miles Davis." In singling out one of his prouder vocal moments of accomplishment on the album, the singer cites the band's smash cover of the Steve Wonder classic 'Higher Ground,' reasoning that the song was "perfect for us...because of the way it translates to our sound. Obviously, the version we do has our own personality interjected into a song that Wonder has already written, but it seemed like the perfect song to us. A definite challenge, but I think we tackled it."

Upon completing the monumental feat of writing and recording *Mother's Milk* and of successfully reinventing themselves via the process, Flea readily acknowledged that "we poured our hearts and souls into this record...It had its good points and bad points... although the good points won out." In addressing how he felt the additions of John Frusciante and Chad Smith had helped to begin the band's next musical revolution, the bassist explained, "we were so hungry, so fresh. These people—Frusciante and Smith—knew what the intention of the RHCP was, but it was their own interpretation that helped us define it."

Lead singer Anthony Kiedis, summarized the band's growth creatively in the course of writing and recording the new LP: "I think what we've created now is just as valid and potent as ever before. We like to expand our musical horizons with every record, whether it is to grow in a melodic direction, or just improve the arrangement of our songs. We're always trying to get better, to change and diversify, and I think we've managed that with this record."

Critically and commercially, the Red Hot Chili Peppers were officially re-introduced to the record buying public on August 16th, 1989. In a reflection of how eager fans were to embrace the band, *Mother's Milk* debuted at a much-improved number 52 on the Billboard Top 200 Album Chart and would quickly sell 500,000 copies, giving the band their first gold record. Moreover, driven by the strength of the band's hit single 'Higher Ground' and its accompanying hit video, which MTV rotated constantly throughout the fall of 1989, the band earned a whole new generation of fans. The band received added attention because of their commercial success as an alternative rock band. They also had a cheering squad among mainstream critics of all fare, with *Playboy Magazine* as one example declaring the band's fourth studio LP as "the most dynamic punk funk connection you're likely to hear for a long time."

Guitar Player Magazine, meanwhile, singled in on guitarist John Frusciante and the ways in which his playing had expanded the band's boundaries stylistically, commenting that the guitarist "plays

49

as if he grew up with one ear glued to a boom box and the other to a Marshall stack. He's a living archive of 70s metal and funk riffs." *All Music Guide* summarized the overall impact of *Mother's Milk* upon the band's long-term career trajectory by recognizing it as "a pivotal album for the Red Hot Chili Peppers…that turned the tide and transformed the band from underground funk-rocking rappers to mainstream bad boys with seemingly very little effort."

Part VI
BloodSugarSexMagik

1991

With the advent of grunge at the start of the 1990s, alternative rock was becoming rock's mainstream commercial. The Red Hot Chili Peppers, along with Jane's Addiction had each established their own subgenre of alt-rock, based off the groundwork both bands had completed respectively in the later 1980s. Jane's Addiction had been the first alternative rock band to kick the commercial door down with *Ritual De La Habitual* in 1990 and their smash single 'Been Caught Stealing.' The next year, the Chili Peppers would pull off one of the greatest heists of commercial market share with their smash fifth studio LP, *BloodSugarSexMagik* and the year's biggest alt-rock single, 'Under the Bridge.' Selling a staggering seven million albums, *BloodSugarSexMagik* would mark the band's transition into mainstream acceptance.

The band's success was fueled in part by guitarist John Frusciante's Hendrix-influenced melodic mazes of beautifully-painted music, Flea and Chad Smith's perfectly fluid yet syncopated rhythm section keeping time with the album's many mystic musical moments, and Anthony Kiedis' transition into a full-on songwriter. The other key to the album's break-through success was the band's decision to collaborate with maverick record producer Rick Rubin, who had tackled every one of the band's influences in the course of his own rise over roughly the same number of years as the Chili Peppers' had been making albums.

Rick Rubin began his ground-breaking, multi-platinum work as co-owner and chief in-house producer at Def Jam Recordings via the Beastie Boys *License to Ill* and Run DMC's *Raising Hell*, as well as successes in rock and metal with break-out albums for Slayer, the Cult, Danzig, and even in pop, producing hits for the Bangles and Roy Orbison as part of the Less Than Zero soundtrack. The producer and band pairing couldn't have been more natural. With every album Rubin had helmed, new ground had been broken in both the genres he had produced and in the commercial growth of the bands' he had produced, without *ever* compromising their artistic roots or integrity in the course of their newfound successes. Rubin was a chameleon, and as diversified a producer in the genres he had recorded. The Chili Peppers were as equally multi-colored in the musical derivatives they blended to form their eclectic sound. The pair was a kindred creative match, whose musical marriage would last the better part of the two decades to follow.

According to lead singer Anthony Kiedis,

> working with Rick was something that turned out to be a magical experience. At first we had a lot of reservations about working with the man because we didn't know him, and he seemed more on the demonic side of life than the explosion of positive energy that the Red Hot Chili Peppers have always been perpetrators of. We didn't know if he would be able to blend in well, what with Slayer and the boiling goat heads of Danzig and all. But he turned out to be a completely open-minded, free-flowing, comforting spirit. If Baron Von Munchausen were able to ejaculate the Red Hot Chili Peppers onto a chessboard, Rick Rubin would be the perfect player for that game.

Delving further into the origins of their collaboration, Flea explained, "we met Rick Rubin when we were getting ready to make *Uplift Mofo Party Plan* in 1987. He came by our rehearsal studio with the Beastie Boys. We had a dark drug cloud over us, so they got uncomfortable and left."

Rubin, for his part, recalled that even from that time they were always incredible musicians, but that doesn't necessarily make a great band." Continuing, Flea noted, "years later, Rick came up after the last show of the *Mother's Milk* tour and said, 'You guys were phenomenal.' We were in a much healthier situation. I talked to him about producing our record, and he said he would love to do it. He wanted to capture who we really were, whereas the producers we worked with in the past were trying to control us. Up until then I was being as wild as I could with my bass. Rick said, 'Be yourself. But it's not about being fancy. It's about serving the song.' I started looking at the song's big picture instead of trying to make fancy bass art pieces."

At the outset of their collaboration, Rubin identified his greatest challenge with the Red Hot Chili Peppers as "breaking down the walls in their own imagination… My job was to break down those boundaries. No band has to fit into a little box. I saw the Chili Peppers as being like the Beach Boys in some ways. They represented Los Angeles, a place of dreams." Flea elaborated on the latter relative to its impact on the overall band musically: "*BloodSugarSexMagik* was the first time that we got down on tape what we really do…We'd never done that before. In the past, we'd always been intimidated by the studio. It would be a tense and alien environment. But that album was more about creating a vibe for us to jam and do our thing in."

That *thing*, as Flea modestly termed it, was the band's most cohesive musical collection of music to date. Capitalizing on and highlighting all their individual musical strengths in sum, Rubin seemed to challenge each band member to push themselves to a more mature place artistically. No greater example of the success of this strategy exists on *BloodSugarSexMagik* than 'Under the Bridge,' which marked the first time that Anthony Kiedis had sung a full-on ballad. The song initially began as a poem for Kiedis, which he described as growing out of the reality that "when you're using drugs, life is pretty lonely. I got clean, but the loneliness didn't go away. I was driving in my car, feeling that loneliness, and started singing the song to myself. I liked what I was singing, so when I got home I taped part of it and started finishing this poem."

Kiedis acknowledged his initial trepidation at the idea of revealing so much of his personal self in the lyrics of the song to the outer world, explaining that Rubin encouraged him by

> visiting me at home where I did my lyric writing, sitting with me on this old '50s couch and saying, 'Let's see what you have.' That's where I first sang, 'Under the Bridge.' It was almost completely written—the arrangement, the verse, and the chorus—as this poem. I had a little melody for each part. Rick convinced me to take 'Under the Bridge' into rehearsal. I was so nervous that my voice cracked when I tried to sing it. The band listened to every last word with a very intense look on their faces. I was about to say, 'We don't have to do this,' when they walked over to their instruments and started finding what they wanted to do with that song.

Rubin reasoned that "it was something that cried for singing, not rapping, and for a melody, not just funk beat, and I said, 'What's this?' and he said, 'Oh, that's not for the Chili Peppers, it's not what we do.'"

Flea further elaborated that

> John and Anthony had a melody and Chad and me added what we could to it. John's mom came in with her church group and sang the background vocals at the end. It was trippy seeing all these women up there singing, 'Under the bridge downtown.' John and I were playing together at the end and had one of those great moments when you're looking at each other and the music's just flowing through you. We both made a little random fill like, 'boo boo da loop' at exactly the same time. The odds of that happening were ten zillion to one. We were like, 'How the fuck did that happen?' We knew that was the take. So I never thought that would be a hit, but I knew that it was good.

Under the Bridge' would become the band's biggest commercial hit to date, highlighting producer Rick Rubin's ear for hits, a talent which Flea qualified as "Rick is a really smart guy…He's very clear-headed and has a good, open-minded view of pop music. Our music is very multicultural, and he has many cultural influences himself. After all, he's produced Run D.M.C., L.L. Cool J, Slayer, the Beastie Boys, and the Bangles. And he just seems to have a natural understanding of what kids like." Anthony Kiedis also seemed to enjoy the fact that Rubin's production-style "let us reveal our music's other sides."

> Preproduction for the album, according to singer Anthony Kiedis, occurred at this amazing rehearsal space called Alleyway. It was run by this biker/hippie couple and decorated with '70s artifacts. We would start playing and every time I heard something that I could relate to, I would say, 'Let's play that again.' John is perfectly nonjudgmental when it comes to creative ideas. He believes that anything that comes to you is meant to be. Our brains work differently, but if you put them together it's like the idiot and the savant. Every time we broke out a guitar or a notebook, we came up with a great song. Then the producer Rick Rubin started coming to rehearsal. He would lay down on the couch with his big-ass beard and appear to take a nap. But he absorbed every note and arrangement and lyrical concept like a sponge.

Elaborating, Flea explained, "we rehearsed and wrote for about six months. Halfway through the process, Rick Rubin got involved… So we'd written for two or three months, then Rick comes and sits through rehearsal for another month or two, and then we go into the studio…His participation is incredibly nonchalant. He just comes by and chills out, sometimes horizontally. He's got a pen and paper and is somewhere between a nap and a meditation. Or sometimes he's on the phone and sometimes he isn't. He notices things about colors and melodies and textures. He's listening to not only the drumbeat itself, but also how it's relating to the bass part. He has an incredible head for arrangement." Rubin recalled, "with the Chili Peppers' *BloodSugarSexMagik* album, we rehearsed for that record nine months. We wanted to cut it very quickly, but it was that advance time that really made the record what it was. It's more about working out the details, the transitions, and the arrangements. This way you have a very good draft before you go into the studio, so you're not trying to write the song in the studio."

Once the band had completed preproduction rehearsals, the band moved from the rehearsal space into a haunted mansion in the Laurel Canyon section of the Hollywood Hills, a move singer Anthony Kiedis described as Rubin's idea, explaining that "when we were in preproduction we were talking to Rick, who's also known as The Bearded Wonder, about how we were going to record, and he was the one that came up with the idea of the house. We were totally gung-ho."

Rubin explained his thinking with the haunted mansion: "the Chili Peppers had made four or five albums before that in their career… and just to take away the feeling that 'Oh, we're making another album, going into the studio doing the same thing we've done every other time,' we rented this big old house, that was empty, kind of like a haunted house kind of thing. We set up everything there, and had the band live there. It was an adventure just making the record. It was different than all of their previous experiences recording. I think there's an energy to it that we wouldn't have gotten had we just gone into a studio the way they had in the past."

According to Flea, the freedom of recording in a house allowed the band to essentially design their version of the ideal recording atmosphere: "when you go to a house like that you can create your own environment. You can make it whatever you want…living, working, eating, having sex, all in the same place, untouched by the outside forces of the world which can really be a distraction when you're trying to focus purely on making music. We could establish the vibe as opposed to a studio where a vibe already exists, with secretaries and owners and lots of extraneous undesirable individuals strolling around the premises." Reinforcing Flea's point, John Frusciante further pointed out that "we sleep here, eat here, and every day we just wake up and start recording…It's a chance not many artists get—to not have to think about bills, answering phones, or shaking hands we don't feel like shaking."

In offering inside the method to his platinum madness, producer Rick Rubin explained,

> I don't listen to the radio or most records that come out today—I just don't like the way they sound. I'd rather listen to the Beatles, the Doors, or Led Zeppelin…A lot of my old favorites, like the Jan & Dean and Beach Boys records, have people singing out of tune or coughing, but they sound great! The technical side is the least important thing to me… I view my role as having more to do with preparing arrangements and getting the best performances out of my artists than with being a great engineer…Producing records is more about the artist and great performances…I don't spend a lot of time getting sounds because mikes in front of amps sound pretty much the same anywhere. The sound really comes from the player's fingers. I just want to hear my artist play his instrument, even if it doesn't sound technically perfect."

Specifically addressing his approach to producing the Red Hot Chili Peppers for the first time, Rubin explained that his focus with the band—in line with his general production philosophy—was on "songwriting and arranging. A lot of what I do is structural, having to do with turnarounds, getting in and out of choruses, putting in space—whatever it takes to make a song sounds like it's not just parts strung together… I started working with the Chili Peppers seven months before we went into the studio." Anthony Kiedis felt the album benefited from the band taking their time in pre-production, explaining that the writing process "was really good fun and a really productive, creative growth spurt for the band as well as for me. There was a lot of growth in the making of that record. For some reason we were in the middle of a record company contract dispute, so we had this extra six months to write music, and there was no pressure of having to make a record since we were in limbo. We kept doing the blue-collar thing and going into the studio and making music. There weren't a lot of changes taking place. It wasn't torturous or destructive. It was a natural evolution. Even the making of it was pretty fun—all under the same roof together."

Describing the physical recording set-up for the album, which was tracked in a haunted Hollywood mansion, singer Anthony Kiedis explained, "we used really old equipment...Our Neve board is from the 50s." Guitarist John Frusciante elaborated, "we all... played... together facing each other downstairs in the living room. The board was...in the next room over, and we mixed all our amps down in the basement...We ran cables up there, and Chad played drums with his hands...I recorded the acoustic guitars in one room, and Anthony does all his vocals from his bedroom. Instead of looking through a window at three sweaty guys frowning in the control room, we're looking out at trees and flowers."

Continuing, the guitarist explained, "the whole house was really just a big, warm, beautiful peaceful place. Not for one minute did we feel any negative energy. Even living together, which could really create tension, turned out perfectly... The number-one ingredient that made '*BloodSugar*' great is that we were really playing along as people, for the most part." Still, according to the bassist, by the time the band began recording their fifth studio album, "we had an intense telepathic thing going musically, anticipating what's going to happen next and being able to really listen to what someone was doing and understand where it was coming from. Playing together and writing together has so much to do with improvisation and that can't happen unless we get inside each other's heads. Our ability to do that has been fully developed."

Being in such a comfortable recording environment only worked to build on that creative comfort zone. Anthony Kiedis noted, "the atmosphere was a luxury that we never really had in the past. There was nothing forced about making this record. We were completely relaxed, which in our opinion, is the key to creative success. The more relaxed you are, the more freely your beautiful spirit can come into the music. When we made our last album, we had been together with this line-up for about three months. This time we were able to develop a fluid musical conversation. We really got to know each other this time...I know we all love what we do. I know it's really fun. I know we're getting better as a band, and the songs over the last few months are the best we've ever written. Everybody goes to work and laughs and rocks out."

According to Flea, the familiarity of living and working under the same roof spoke to the band's comfort level with one another musically by that point, allowing them to expand the creative boundaries in terms of stripping down to basics: "nothing was recorded to a click...It was a very peaceful time." Kiedis added years later, "Rick turned out to be the best producer we could ever have hoped to have...He's very intelligent, very emotionally in-tune with hardcore, soulful music. He knows how to extrapolate the best and most relaxed natural performance of a band without changing them...He makes subtle, little, well-focused, well-thought out changes in the arrangement in songs and basically lays there and les you do your thing."

Producer Rick Rubin spoke to the *natural* method of his and the band's approach to recording: "we'd mixed fifteen Chili Peppers songs so far, and I don't think we've used any reverb yet. It's amazing how dry and personal this record is. What you hear is what you get—there's not a lot of trickery. A lot of people want the biggest sound, with wall of guitar and huge drums. But I don't think those things matter...The 'newest sounds' have a tendency to sound old when the next new sound comes along. But a grand piano sounded great 50 years ago and will sound great 50 years from now. AC/DC's *Highway to Hell* came out 12 years ago but could have been recorded yesterday. Same with the Zeppelin stuff. I try to make records that have that timeless quality. And as time goes on, I find that I like the organic sound of everyone playing together in the same room, facing each other. If you don't worry about the perfection of individual parts or perfection of sound, you get the best performance."

Elaborating further, John Frusciante explained,

> Womb' is a very good word. We didn't ever leave the place—you just woke up, relaxed, took a few deep breaths, put a grape in your ear and started making music. Very easy. Very beautiful. Concentrating on doing nothing. I don't really care about my own creativity. I didn't even pay attention to my own playing. I just care about my life. I wasn't even listening to the guitar or how I was making it sound during the recording sessions. I just enjoy playing music with people I love. You don't pay attention to what you're playing, you just look into the other guy's eyes, or at his hands, or his knee, or whatever…This is the fastest we've ever done a record. We zipped right though the basics, twenty-five songs. We were tight as hell—we totally got inside each other's heads and became one being. Our music is so much more colorful than in the past, and I'm so happy about it. I never took anything so seriously in my life… It's an entity made by the four of us jumping out of our bodies into a cosmic swell. We've all grown out of love and admiration for each other.

That, according to the band, the house was allegedly haunted added an entirely different vibe to the recording process. Flea cited the recording of one of the album's tracks, 'They're Red Hot,' a Robert Johnson cover, as an example of the haunting influencing the recording process. As the bassist explained, "when we recorded the Robert Johnson song…up on a hill behind the house up at like two in the morning. It was a hot summer night. We had chairs set up and all our acoustic guitars out there. Chad was playing with his hands. We started playing and it felt so fucking good. Right at the end of the track these people drove down the street in Laurel Canyon. You can hear them if you've got headphones. They're like, 'Wee-hoo!' reveling in their partyness. We thought we were in a haunted house when we were making this record. Noises like that just added to the whole ambiance…There were times when I thought that I felt something. These ghost experts did a séance and said there were ghosts all over the place. I liked the idea that there were ghosts. One time this big plant leaf started waving up and down, even though there wasn't any breeze. John thought he could hear a woman making sexual noises."

Delving further into the depths of the house's supernatural presence, Anthony Kiedis noted,

> there were ghosts everywhere. They came out on about four of the photos we took for an album cover session—these floating nebulous shapes. The pictures were taken with a red filter and anytime ectoplasmic experts are attempting to photograph ghosts they always do it with infrared. The photographer, Gus Van Zandt, did it, and he wasn't even trying to capture a ghost. Keep in mind that the house was built in 1917. It had been owned by gangsters, the Beatles had taken LSD there as a foursome, Jimi Hendrix stayed there, people were born and died there… it's deeply saturated with history. It's obvious to us that there's a real world of spirits that people just aren't tuned into. We were accepting of the fact that we were living among them. We weren't there to be obtrusive. We were there to make music and to coexist in what was really their house more than ours."

John Frusciante reflected that on one occasion during the album's recording, "I was sleeping right here about a week after we moved in, and I heard the sound of a woman having sex, but there was definitely no woman in the house. And other people who worked on the project have seen things." Rubin felt the house was a perfect atmosphere in which to record the album because "they had made either four or five albums before that in their career, and just to take away the feeling that, oh, we're making another album, going into the studio doing the same thing we've done every other time, we rented this big old house, that was empty, kind of like a haunted house type of thing. We set up everything there, and had the band live there. It was an adventure just making the record. It was different than all of their previous experiences recording. I think there's an energy to it that we wouldn't have gotten had we just gone into a studio the way they had in the past. So sometimes just setting up another environment makes for a more interesting session."

Delving into the band's songwriting process for the album, singer Anthony Kiedis described that the band's goal, as with every album, was to grow creatively, explaining, "Nothing is anything like what we'd done previously. The whole point of being a band is to constantly grow and change and explore new musical territory…to get better and increase your ability to express yourself, so that what you're feeling comes out in music. With some of the slower songs, which may come as a surprise to our fans, that's just how we were feeling and we had the ability this time to express those feelings." *BloodSugarSexMagik* marked the first time fans had heard virtually anything acoustic from the Chili Peppers, and it showed a new side entirely to the listeners in the process, largely thanks to John Frusciante.

Explaining the songwriting process for the band's acoustic material, beginning with "Breaking the Girl," bassist Flea explained that "it started off with John Frusciante getting these chords together with his acoustic guitar in his house in Mt. Olympus. Anthony wrote those words and sang a beautiful melody. When we got to the studio, the drummer Chad Smith started doing that really loose, beautiful beat on it. We went to the junkyard and got a bunch of stuff to play the rhythm on. I always wanted to do that because our when our ex-drummer Cliff Martinez was in Captain Beefheart's band, he would go get car hoods and metal pipes and buckets to play on. It was really fun."

John Frusciante explained his inspiration for "Breaking the Girl": "when I was working on 'Breaking The Girl' I listened a lot to Led Zeppelin. I especially liked 'Friends.' I also played a 12-string back them. That's where the idea to 'Breaking The Girl' came from. I took the chords of the chorus from the book on Duke Ellington. I tried to learn one song from this book and played three chords of a song, which has at least 50 chords. Based on these three chords and some additional stuff, I wrote our song…I did draw a lot of inspiration from other music and imagined to comprise the style of some of my favorite guitarists in my work."

Addressing the general presence of the band's softer side on the album, Frusciante explained that "at the time of *BloodSugarSexMagik* Flea was already going in the direction of doing less sleep and playing simpler, and I think he just got more and more interested in blending with the whole thing as possible. For me simplicity has always been my mind concept when we've been in the studio." That stripped-down methodology allowed the band to collectively explore other sides of its musical personality. The bassist reasoned, "on the majority of rock records you don't hear a guitar or drums or bass. You hear a bunch pf processed synthesized shit. That's all because it's a wall of sound…A recording studio creation. This record is very minimal and it's very live. When I hear it, I get a picture of a hand hitting a guitar, a string vibrating. This is four guys playing music. That took us awhile to learn to do. There are so many options in the studio; you've got to know what you want. We were real careful not to do anything unless it helped the song, which meant keeping that band feel all the time."

To gain any truly in-depth understanding of the Chili Peppers' songwriting style, one must first go to the source of much of their structural material: the relationship between bassist Flea and guitarist John Frusciante. Frusciante reasoned, "you can't force inspiration." The band tended to create the skeletons for most of their songs out of live jams: "most of our songs are created from jamming...Sometimes I bring the entire guitar parts for a song along and the others add their parts...Things such as duration or arrangement are of course developed by all of us together... During...jams, Flea sometimes played the same bass line for over half an hour, and I tried various guitar parts on top of it. Flea loves it to put himself into a hypnotic groove. I join in and as soon as he has caught me I will play one part after the other each one giving Flea's bass line a completely different flavor. Those songs don't sound like the bass is playing the same part all the time, but he does...We generally develop songs as a band. Sometimes we record our jam sessions. Anthony goes through those tapes and a week or a month later he presents us bits and pieces of those tapes going 'This groove is hot. We should write a song around it.' We write tons of stuff and when Anthony dances across the room doing his moves it feels great."

Kiedis describes an example of the latter in action with the writing of another smash from the album, *Give it Away*: "it was a hot summer day in the rehearsal studio. Flea started hitting that big heavy slide bass line. I had been thinking about this concept Nina Hagen planted in my mind. She was my girlfriend when I was 20 years old and believed that the more she gave, the more she received. When I got sober, I realized that sobriety revolved around giving something away in order to maintain it. So this idea of *Give It Away* was tornado-ing in my head for a while. When Flea started hitting that bass line, that tornado just came out of my mouth."

Producer Rick Rubin seemed to favor the band's fluid song-writing style, feeling it was most honestly in line with the way the band interacted at its musical core:

> their love and appreciation of music, and the musicianship between the players in that band, the level of interactivity in their playing—I don't think there are any other big bands that do that... that really *jam*. They really do. They can play anything, and they *listen* to each other, which is so

rare. A lot of bands, people just play their parts, but the Chili Peppers are truly an interactive band, kind of in the way that musicians might have been in the '60s. That's one of the reasons that there were so many bands back then; it was a different kind of musicianship. It was about playing together, playing off each other, and complementing each other. Really, John Frusciante and Flea have this kind of magical interaction, almost like a psychic relationship.

As a guitarist, John Frusciante is rock 'n' roll's Van Gogh—his musical genius was internally maddening and would lead him to metaphorically cut off his own ear for a few years before he recognized his own relevance in making alternative rock work, just as the Chili Peppers' and their fans would after his absence. Prior thereto, the musical foundation he laid in the course of *BloodSugarSexMagik* would teach a listening generation how to feel melody as naturally and helplessly as they did emotion. Beneath Anthony Kiedis' interpretation of each largely teenage fan's collage of confusion, anxiety, love, pain, redemption, and every related emotion along that spectrum would serve as the stage where each emotion's character played themselves out into a resolution by the point each song's completion. Each of Frusciante's songs were portraits, every note a stroke of genius that adds a new strand of interpretation to the mystery that is music to the naked ear.

Once covered in the fabric of his melodic warmth, Frusciante possessed the ability to strip that comfort away, or quilt his listeners in the warmth of its opposite—if Kiedis' lyrics required it. Either way, Frusciante was the safety net for the band's brilliant musical wanderings. Discussing some of his derivative influences in context of his playing style on *BloodSugarSexMagik*, Frusciante cited:

> Johnny Marr of The Smiths, for example, Siouxie & The Banshees, Matthew Ashman of Bow Wow Wow or Bernard Sumner of New Order and Joy Division none of those were great guitarists, technically speaking, but they

stood out due to their individual way of playing, something that makes them unique. But wait the more I think about it, the more influences come to my mind. For example, a song by Nightmares on Wax, I think, which is on some Warped compilation. You find it in 'Time', which is a b-side on the first single. When I pinch from others it's important to either take the technical aspect or the feeling, but never both at the same time. If you develop this further from there adding your own signature, you will put enough distance between you and the original. I never aimed at being original, I just happened to stumble into it.

Amazingly, for as sophisticated-sounding as his play was throughout the album, according to the guitarist,

on *BloodSugar*...I was capable of playing much more than I did...I was being very careful to not think and to play from somewhere else other than my brain activity to play guitar. I would shut off my brain and let my fingers just go and listen to the bass and the drums, and not really listen to myself except the sound coming back from my own guitar...Not that I think it's bad guitar playing...But I was so concerned with doing everything in one take, I didn't really take any chances in the studio. With a couple of exceptions, I knew exactly what I was going to do. I think at that time I'm just completely improvising, and every solo has a real spontaneous, even haphazard feel to it. I'm not putting down my guitar playing, I just feel like I was capable of a whole lot of things instead of just cramming in every bit of technique that I possibly could.

Continuing, Frusciante explained,

around the time we started writing *BloodSugar*, I finally put aside those guitarists' styles, and I forgot about what's technically good. I thought, for example, that Keith Richards makes music that connects with so many people, and he plays in such a simple way, so why don't I pick a variety of people along those lines who play simple but do something that makes a beautiful sound that affects people emotionally? For me, that was a new way of thinking that to a while adjusting to. So by the time we recorded *BloodSugar*, I still felt as though I was doing a balancing act and I didn't really feel comfortable with what I was doing, which is probably a good thing... When I was playing guitar, I would play this game with myself. I would say, 'I'm going to leave my body now. I'm going to be holding the guitar and recording what I'm playing, but I'm not going to be here.' In time I just started having this natural belief in these spiritual forces that were possessing my body. I'd always had voices in my head as a kid, but now I started getting a really excessive amount of voices in my head. They were having conversations with me. Telling me about the future. They'd say something was going to happen in two minutes. And whatever it was they said would really happen. They would do these things to show me that they were in tune with the future and could see the future. Because the future has already happened many times. They don't live in a dimension that has time, but they sort of feed off the energies of people who do live in dimensions that have time.

Flea qualified the latter: "John is playing much freer and thinking less. I loved John's playing on *Mother's Milk,* but now he's so pure and spontaneous. He never considers doing something again and again—he'll just record maybe one overdub. He likes capturing the natural feeling on tape." Continuing, Frusciante explained, "almost all the solos are first takes and some of them were cut along with the basics, like 'My Lovely Man' and the first solo on 'Funky Monks.' On '*Funky Monks*' I played everything without a pick, even the solo. I've been playing that way more and more lately—in fact, I haven't used a pick in weeks now…I was thinking 'rubber band.' I've gotten more into those kinds of rhythms, because they sound more natural than really straight stuff. The second part of the solo is one of the few fast parts on the album. I though of it as a parody of a rock star solo. The intro has electric guitars not plugged in, just miced acoustically. It's the same thing Dave Navarro of Jane's Addiction does on *Been Caught Stealing*, though Snakefinger did it first."

Frusciante's preference for simplicity extends not only to his playing, but also to his equipment. The guitarist explained,

> I like to keep things simple. Those MESA/Boogie amps were too hard for me to understand. For most of the basics, I used two Marshalls: a guitar head for edge and a bass head for punch and low end. I split the signal with a DOD stereo chorus pedal. For some overdubs I used a Fender H.O.T. practice amp, but for a lot of parts, even solos, I just went straight into the board. You can get amazing, funky tones that way. In fact, a lot of my distortion is from overdriving the board. My main guitar was a '58 Strat, though I used a Les Paul reissue on a couple of things. I also have a '57 Strat, which someone had screwed up by putting on those big stupid frets that everyone uses these days. I vomited and told them to make it fretless… Some people think those big frets help your vibrato, but I make a point of using as little vibrato as possible, though I might do it more if I had long, pretty black hair. And I didn't use any whammy bar.

Delving further into the technical side of what guitars were used on various songs throughout the recording of the album, Frusciante explained, "I used a Coral Electric Sitar on '*BloodSugarSexMagik*,' and I used an old Gibson lap steel for the solo at the beginning of 'The Righteous and The Wicked.' My acoustic is a newish Martin steel-string. But my favorite guitar in the world is my old, fucked-up Fender Jaguar. The strings are all crusty, and the notes crap out when you bend them. I used it to write most of the music, and I became really attached to it…My only effects were an Electro-Harmonix Big Muff and an Ibanez Wah. I like the Ibanez because you can make adjustments without taking it apart, and it has a bass setting that sounds more like an envelope filter than a wah. I used that on 'Naked in the Rain.'…I went direct into the board and overdrove the channel input for the solo to 'Suck My Kiss.'"

While Frusciante focused on keeping things technically and musically simplified in his own playing style on the album, Flea's playing was his most poetic and sophisticated to date, showcasing the multiple levels and layers of brilliance as a bassist. Already wildly established and considered among the top bassists in the world by that point via his thematic focus on wild, roller-coasters of funk throughout the band's first four albums, on *BloodSugarSexMagik*, Flea seemed to focus on textures—painting a portrait alongside Frusciante. He added his own colors to each song, in a blend that, according to the bassist, allowed him to "these amazing collages that sounded so good and had so much emotional value. I've learned that it's all in the artist, not in the tools that are used. Some people are so proud of the fact that they play these screaming macho lead guitars, and they think it's terrible that someone would use a machine…That feeling of having just bottom without hearing definite notes came out of what the hip-hop guys were doing with their Roland 808 drum machine. I used to be totally anti-drum machine because I felt that anything computerized was wrecking music be getting away from pure human emotion."

Rubin recalled,

> when I started working with the Chili Peppers the first time, which was on the *BloodSugarSexMagik* album. Up until that time, Flea's bass playing was a particular style. He was famous for it, considered one of the best bass players in the world because of it. But when we started working together, that bass playing that made him one of the best didn't necessarily serve the songs in the best way. It was more about the bass being great. And, the song is more important than the bass…I think, starting with that record, he changed the way he played. Not that it was so different stylistically, but it was more about playing the parts that supported the song. Instead of playing the parts that he liked the best or that were the coolest…It was a very interesting part of the change in the Chili Peppers' sound, from being a, let's say, 'traditional' funk band to being more of a songwriting band.

Sharing a musical canvas with the bassist, according to Frusciante, began with the guitarist "consciously decided to aim at playing behind Flea, keeping my sound clean and using my distortion pedal only for solos. I wanted to keep my solos as minimal as possible and wanted to play in a more spatial way. I wanted to create more room. The guitarists that I then considered to be good models were Matthew Ashman of Bow Wow Wow, who's also playing with a rather 'busy' bass guitarist, and Andy Sumner of The Police. I considered myself more and more as support for Flea and Chad. This way I discovered exactly what I'm good at. And the most fascinating thing about it was this: Since I began to retreat from the foreground, creativity simply started to pour out of me thus automatically putting me into the fore at the same time however in a deeper way."

Continuing, the guitarist recalled,

> Flea, on the other hand, also became more simple, more delicate and useful for me to play with. Somehow everyone in the band suddenly took off into this direction. Meanwhile all of this is so well-developed and steady between us that I don't have to think about it at all for me things just flow…It is good to display opposites. I remember a good exercise we did during the time of *BloodSugar* to practice playing together. While Flea played a complex funky and syncopated rhythm I tried to fill the holes with chords and to kind of play in between Flea. I think it is important to create new rhythms. If someone plays something and you want to join the jam you should try to find a different rhythm, one that is part of what the other plays and that supports whatever he started out with. This way you create something completely new. Sometimes we play harmonies that suit each other and sometimes we play stuff that is totally apart…Sometimes, we both play exactly the same rhythm but are adding different notes. The combination of this produces a double stop, which in itself implies chords. I don't have a clue which ones. We simply face each other and listen just like Fugazi who often come up with chords in which guitar and bass play different notes."

Delving further into his conceptually stripped-down playing style on *BloodSugarSexMagik*, the bassist explained,

> I consciously avoided anything busy or fancy. I tried to get small enough to get inside the song, as opposed to stepping out and saying, 'Hey, I'm Flea, the bitchin' bass player.' I can play fast things that make bass players say 'Wow!' but it's better to imply your technique with something simple… I hardly slap at all on the new record, aside

from 'Naked in the Rain.' You know, I was reading this Bass Player interview with Kim Gordon of Sonic Youth, who I really respect. She said she loved funk bass but hated the way white guys play it, because they've turned it into this macho-jock thing. As I read that, I knew I was responsible for that tendency. But on the new record I don't do any of that—I try to play simply and beautifully. And I hope she doesn't hate me, 'cause I think she's great... I remember trying to play very simply. In the past, I've played some things just to be a bitchin' player, but that wasn't the overall attitude this time around."

Frusciante concurs with Flea's musical reasoning, arguing, "you can get just as many 'wows' that way. And after you've heard a million bass players rip off Flea's slap thing, what's the point of continuing to do it?" For his part, singer Anthony Kiedis thought that the stripped-down approach grew out of the fact that "the Red Hot Chili Peppers have always been driven by the power of funk, since day one. On this record we took the time to simplify everything that we do, to give it more room to breathe. Funk can be a simple as one note or it can be as complicated as a barrage of fifty notes in three seconds...Flea—already the No. 1 bass-popper of his generation—began to express the other side of his playing."

Flea detailed the gear he used in the course of tracking *BloodSugar-SexMagik*:

> I started using Music Man basses because they're good and inexpensive. When I could afford one, I got a Spector, but it kept shorting out. I went back to the Music Mans because they're so simple and pure, but I've had problems keeping their necks straight—I had to constantly adjust them on tour. For this record I wanted something really good for the studio with a variety of sounds, so I got a WAL, which I used for most of the 4-string songs, though I used the Music Man for 5-string and fretless stuff. I still think Music Man basses look coolest. Every amp I've ever

had breaks. For this album I used a Galien-Krueger head with MESA/Boogie cabinets. I'm not especially into them—they're just the shit I happen to play through now. There's no effects except for an old Mu-Tron on '*Sir Psycho Sexy*' and some envelope filter on a couple of things. I used a combination of mike and direct for most of the album, though I used direct only on a few things.

The critical and commercial success of the Red Hot Chili Peppers' fifth studio album would rocket them into worldwide superstardom, turning their cult following and funk-metal subgenre into a mainstream musical medium that would become arguably the most lasting and influential of the decade. Consider *Rolling Stone Magazine's* review of the album "the pummeling '*Give It Away*' and the incendiary '*Suck My Kiss*' established a template for rock punctuated by the beatcentric relentlessness of hip-hop that would be appropriated by everyone from Limp Bizkit to Dr. Dre." More important however, were the leaps of personal artistic growth within the band's sound "the more introverted material—the lashing, triple-meter 'Breaking the Girl' and Kiedis' drug confessional 'Under the Bridge'—that revealed new dimensions. The rhythm section displayed a growing curiosity about studio texture and nuance."

Clearly, the magazine had been studying the Chili Peppers creative evolution for years and noted Rubin's presence as producer on the album as the catalyst that allowed the band to make the breakthrough to the true musical enlightenment everyone watching and listening felt they'd always been capable: "insisting on airborne melodies, filtering the rhythmic rumble down to a brutal essence, the acclaimed Beastie Boys producer had changed the Chilis' dynamic."

The change would be permanent, both in its affect on the genre of alternative rock in terms of the boundaries the album proved could be pushed without compromising artistic integrity or commercial potential and on the band in that they now set the bar, and could raise it whenever they were next ready. Unfortunately, that growth would be temporarily stunted when guitarist John Frusciante abruptly quit the band in 1993, at the height of the band's wildly successful world tour in support of *BloodSugarSexMagik*, which by that time had moved over five million units.

The group would eventually hire Jane's Addiction guitarist Dave Navarro to replace Frusciante—to the degree it was possible. Regardless, the success of the band's breakout album, according to lead singer Anthony Kiedis, revealed to the band that we weren't just communicating to a small circle of friends in Los Angeles and New York anymore. It might not swim with the current, but it's out there—putting something beautiful into a stream that gets a little stagnant at times...The album's success opened a new avenue for us. Suddenly, even more than before, everything was okay under the Red Hot Chili Peppers' umbrella. The album's successes seemed to producer Rick Rubin as the only possible outcome, simply out of the fact that, as Rubin reasoned, "we put everything we have into it all the time, whatever it takes...If we're going to do it, let's aim for greatness...because if it's not going to be great, I'd much rather go swimming."

Following Frusciante's departure, the band was metaphorically treading water, trying to stay afloat in a sea of speculation throughout the industry. The drafting of ex-Jane's Addiction guitarist Navarro three years later, along with their reteaming with Rubin, would quiet naysayers. In 1994, the band—once again with Rubin at the helm—entered the studio to begin working on their sixth studio album, *One Hot Minute.*

Part VII
One Hot Minute

1995

Following John Frusciante's departure in 1993, the band released one last hit from the guitarist on 'Soul to Squeeze,' as well as a Hits retrospective from their first decade together with 'What Hits?' before going into creative hibernation. According to Frusciante in hindsight, the departure had been fueled in part by "a certain amount of tension between me and Anthony then that isn't there now. To me, that's what makes this time even better than the *BloodSugar* period; the whole band was united on this album. When one of us has a problem with one of the others, we always talk about it; we get it out in the open. Nobody holds a grudge against anybody. We didn't work that way at the time of *BloodSugar*, and it ended up biting us in the ass. That as a big part of my reason for quitting the band. Anthony and I just couldn't see eye to eye. Back then we were both the kind of people who tended to blame anyone other than themselves for what's wrong."

The group would not emerge again until Woodstock in the summer of 1994, debuting the new line-up with Dave Navarro for the first time. Though the band's tenure with the new guitarist would last—figuratively speaking—as long as the title of the album they made together, it seemed a fitting pairing at the time given where alternative rock had landed by the mid-1990s. Without Jane's Addiction or Kurt Cobain, the Chili Peppers were one of only a handful of superstar bands—alongside Pearl Jam, Soundgarden, and the Stone Temple Pilots—keeping Alternative Rock alive as a viable commercial entity. Though four years had lapsed between the release of *BloodSugarSexMagik* and *One Hot Minute*, fans seemed patient given the widely-publicized exit of John Frusciante and

Anthony Kiedis' suffering from, what had been reported through-out rock news as, an extreme case of writer's block.

Dave Navarro's decision to join the band had been motivated by what the guitarist described as a situation in which "everything that encompasses who I am and who I've been in my life has been brought to this band in an amicable way. I think that I come from a slightly different place, musically speaking. These guys are percussive and sharp edged, to use an expression that Flea has come up with, and I'm into melodic and ethereal sounds. And I think that the combination has really worked and given birth to something really new." Anthony Kiedis, for his part, viewed the benefit of Navarro's addition as simply a situation in which "Dave had something that nobody else had and that was Dave."

To fans, it seemed like the next-best-thing at the time, even if it was generally acknowledged that most rock fans would have preferred if Jane's Addiction had never broken up, and that Frusciante would have never left the Chili Peppers to begin with. They were not the same band without him, something in hindsight that Flea conceded "the contrast made a big difference. John was a huge fan of the band when he joined, so it wasn't a big change for us. He did come into his own aesthetic as time went on, and he had a huge amount to do with the sound of the band, but Dave's coming from his own trip—the Jane's Addiction thing in particular, which was very different from the Chili Peppers… John was the missing link, only with him were we able to create an album like *BloodSugarSexMagik*…It's just that chemistry to this particular band is a must, and that chemistry exists with John, and for him not to be there—granted, we got a beautiful person and a wonderful musician in Dave Navarro, but the chemistry was different and it wasn't really the right chemistry for us…It had its ups and downs…The record is what it is, though: a document of that time…That's no slight towards Dave because I feel real lucky to have played with him during that time—in some strange way it kept us together during that period."

With Navarro part of the fold, the band's first order of business, according to Anthony Kiedis, wasn't to rush into the studio, but rather "getting to know each other and hanging out together and working on music. No one told us when it was finished because we knew when it was finished. If it takes ten years to make a record, then that's how long it takes. This record took us a year to make, and it's a good thing that it took that long, because if it would have taken less time, it wouldn't be what it is now. There's a natural flow of creative unity and that doesn't happen according to a schedule or a deadline."

Flea concurred, reasoning that focusing on deadlines or expectations would have gotten in the way of the music: "the commercial success of a record is really not our concern. Our concern is trying to make the most honest music that we can. We're really proud of this record. We think we've grown a lot and made an album that sounds different than anything we've ever done. And whatever the world wants to do with it is fine." For Navarro, the focus seemed to be on fitting into the band's sound without compromising his own. He described the writing and recording process as one that was "different for me because for the past 13 years I've worked by myself, and now I have the input of these guys. But it works to the fullest potential and we've come up with something really exciting and new and we hope everyone loves it."

The result was a complicated, emotional record. Flea seemed to feel his role as bassist was to keep it simple, as he was expanding—perhaps out of some necessity—into other roles within the band:

> I've put less emphasis on the bass…I'm trying to improve as a songwriter as well…I was trying to play simply on *BloodSugar* because I had been playing too much prior to that, so I thought, I've really got to chill out and play half as many notes. When you play less, it's more exciting—there's more room for everything. If I do play something busy, it stands out, instead of the bass being a constant onslaught of notes. Space is good. I think my playing on *One Hot Minute* is even simpler; I just wanted to play shit that sounded good. I thrashed through the recording and didn't care about the parts being perfect. It's not that I don't love the bass passionately anymore—I just felt I'd been getting too many accolades for being 'Joe Bass Player.'…I do consider myself fortunate to have achieved popularity as a bassist, but I felt there was too much emphasis being placed on playing technique, as opposed to just playing music. So before we recorded this album, I spent more time strumming an acoustic guitar than I did playing bass. To me, my bass parts are more incidental to the song now, because I'm thinking less as a bass player and more as a songwriter.

The latter role, in particular, took on a larger emphasis for Flea in the course of writing *One Hot Minute*: "I wrote almost all of the music on the record. So you've expanded beyond writing only grooves? I've always had a major hand in writing, but on some of the *One Hot Minute* songs, I wrote the chords and the melody and most of the words. I wrote a lot of the lyrics on 'Deep Kick' and 'Transcending,' for example." Describing the process by which he and Navarro demoed song ideas in the course of writing the album, Flea explained, "mostly I'd play acoustic guitar and come up with the chords and melody, and Dave would take my simple guitar part and play it in his magical Navarro way. Or, I would have a bass line, and Dave would think of a guitar part to go with it."

Amazingly, the bassist had only begun learning guitar a short time before writing began in principle. Seeming to have grown partially out of an urging by producer Rick Rubin, Flea reflected, "I started a couple of months before we began making this record. Rick Rubin gave me a Martin acoustic, and I bought a Neil Young songbook to learn chords. Playing guitar has definitely helped me as a songwriter; instead of thinking in terms of bass lines and grooves, which is an amazing way to think, I now think about chord progressions and melodies. It's another musical dimension for me."

Writing was one aspect of creating the new album the band had to adjust to with Navarro in the fold, but recording proved to be an adjustment all its own. For Flea and Navarro, who as a duo had already scored one hit together playing on Alanis Morrisette's smash 'You Oughta Know,' there was some foundation to build on. Still, once recording got underway, according to Flea, other adjustments were required due to the fact that "Dave Navarro is intensely different from John Frusciante. When we recorded *BloodSugar*, John played all his tracks once and maybe overdubbed a few solos, so the whole record was very spontaneous. Dave is really into the studio; he would spend weeks on every song, put something like 15 tracks of guitar on every tune, and weed through it in the mix. Dave's sound is more layered and 'effecty' than John's, which was like, boom-play it dry and leave it alone. Also, Dave and I are very different musically. He'll often play some '70s rock song, and most of the time I don't even know who did it, but I'll start playing along-and to me it's ridiculous. But our differences create our music."

Navarro himself refused to place the music the band was writing and recording into any one niche or category, explaining that to do so wouldn't work because "I don't think there is a categorization that fits. I think if we categorize our music, it leaves us in a closed position where we're trying to open doors." This logic seemed to make sense given the band was essentially starting over, and according to Kiedis, being open to all possibilities was key to their growth as a revitalized creative entity, explaining that "we've always been emotionally diverse, and I think that the longer that we're alive, the more aware of ourselves we become and that gives us the ability to express ourselves more clearly."

Taking that philosophy one step further, the front man seemed eager to avoid analyzing too much about the band's creative process, perhaps because it was still a mystery; or alternately because, from the singer's point of view, describing the process would be fruitless: "songwriting is a state of mind, it's a state of spirit. It happens every way imaginable...I hate talking about songs. I really hate analyzing our music. It takes all the fun out of it; it takes the mystery and the beauty out of it. We work on songs and we record them for people to hear and it isn't our place to sit there and try to give detailed explanations of how a song came to be or what it's about…There's no formula. No song is ever written the same way twice. It happens with a bass line. It happens with a guitar part. It happens with a drum part. It happens with a vocal part. It happens when we get together and work and there is no secret to it. It's just an intangible factor."

While Kiedis seemed to prefer to keep the band's process for writing secret, Flea was much more up front and open about the adjustments he had been making as a musician and songwriter in the process, noting that he was "trying to figure out new sounds and get my hands and mind to be coordinated in a beautiful, flowing way. My dynamic has changed—I really want to improve as a bass player…I'm jamming on grooves and bass lines and trying to find new ones…I like hearing the bass when it's really locking in with the drums. I like it simple. I like it when it makes you want to fuck-that warm, good feeling. Very seldom do I enjoy bass playing that takes center stage…Plenty of bass players have fancy chops, but they don't make you feel any emotions. You don't feel anger, fear, or love. That's what I call 'all flash and no smash.'"

Delving into the writing of some of the specific songs on *One Hot Minute*, Flea explained that the songs came together out of a mix of jamming and concentrated songwriting: "to me, this is the least jam-oriented record we've made. I mean, we definitely jammed on the ideas, but there's only one groove on the whole album that came from a jam, 'Deep Kick.' The rest of it came from my sitting down with a guitar or bass and saying, 'Check this out, guys.'" Flea for one seemed to feel open-mindedness was the key to making the album's songs work, reasoning, "I think being a good songwriter requires being in touch with all the emotions and stuff that are flying through the air around you."

Flea also addressed the creation of some of the specific songs on the album, beginning with 'Aeroplane':

> I was sitting in my garage with a bass Louis Johnson gave me—a Treker Louis Johnson Signature 4-string—and I started playing that '70s funk line. The bass had light strings on it and had that whacka-whackita sound. It's kind of a 'been done' groove, but it's nice and Anthony liked it. The chorus part was one of those things where we were stuck; sometimes when we're looking for another part, I'll have no idea what I'm going to do, but I'll say, 'What about this?' It's all sliding on the E-string. Actually, 'Aeroplane' was the only song I was worried about—I thought it sounded like another stupid white boy trying to be funky! I put it out anyway, but it's the one thing I'd go back and fix. When I played it live in the studio with the band, the bass didn't record right for some reason, so it was one of the few things I had to overdub. The part kept feeling stiff to me, as if it wasn't my day; I wasn't flowing with the drums. I wanted to redo it, but Rick said, 'It's cool.' 'Coffee Shop' is chock full of bass stuff, including a solo. It's funny—'Coffee Shop' would never have been a song if it weren't for this effect called the BassBalls.
>
> I started playing with it one morning in Hawaii, and it had the most amazing underwater, Bootsy kind of sound—and it also had this siren effect going on. But when we got to L.A. to start recording, the box never made the sound again. I got so mad, I crushed it! I almost didn't even want to record the song, because to me, it was all about that bass sound. I ended up using a Boss Dynamic Filter on the record. In the solo, it sounds as if you're ripping the strings off the fingerboard. We didn't know what to do at the end, so I said, 'I'll solo.' I played the track once, and I wanted to fix it later because I thought it sucked, but I never did. 'Pea,' your bass-and-vocals solo piece, features an acoustic bass

guitar. Yeah-it's a Sigma acoustic. There's not much to say about 'Pea.' I mean, it's just a song I wrote...The ending of 'One Big Mob' has a heavy feel. That song was actually part of a 12-minute movement. The end was the intro to another song called 'Stretch You Out,' which is more of a funk thing, but we didn't put it on the record. It's too bad, because bass players would probably like that tune more than any other song on the album. I think we'll put it out as a B-side. 'Walkabout' is built around the bass, especially the verses. I had gone to see the Spike Lee movie Crooklyn, which has this cool '70s funk soundtrack. I came home, picked up my bass, and started playing that verse line. I wrote the intro at rehearsal—it was another one of those 'What about this?' things. 'Transcending' centers around a twisted b7 bass riff. I play the root and the b7, which ring at the same time, and then I play the 4th and bend it up while I keep plucking. I wrote that part on my acoustic bass guitar while I was sitting on the beach in Hawaii, before I decided we should all write there.

In terms of the physical atmosphere in which the album was recorded, Anthony Kiedis explained, "for the last record, *Blood-SugarSexMagik*, we all moved into a house and lived together while we recorded. But I think it would be pretty stupid to try to recreate something we did a long time ago, so we tried to do something new this time. We went to Hawaii for three months and lived and wrote songs and played around together."

Even though the physical environment was new, Kiedis and company seemed to take great comfort in having the familiarity of producer Rick Rubin working behind the recording console. According to Kiedis "Rick...was with us the whole time and his influence was greatly appreciated. He's our friend as well as our producer, so we have a great rapport and it was a rewarding experience as always to work with him."

While Flea seemed eager to understate the funk that had historically dominated the band's signature sound in favor of more subtle, melodic explorations, front man Anthony Kiedis seemed to speak up on the style's behalf to reassure fans that "funk is so subtle that obviously it eludes any shallow interpretation of what funk is. There's funk all over this record, but we don't necessarily sound black or white. We sound like people connected to a universal energy, inspired to play music that knows no color." Flea seemed to feel confident that all of the band's traditional styles would be aptly represented musically on the album, while in the same time the band—as a byproduct of its natural musical evolution—would inevitably incorporate new ones. As the bassist seemed to view it, "the Red Hot Chili Peppers have always run a pretty wide spectrum throughout our careers and obviously through the years we have become more capable to express that range."

To capture his bass sound, Flea used "an Alembic bass for most of the record. It was the bass I had in the studio, so I was like, 'Let's record, let's rock.' The Alembic isn't as in-my-face as the Music Man, but the high notes are as loud as the low ones, from the bottom of the neck to the top, which is a problem on the Music Man. I probably could have used the StingRay for the entire album, but when we go to record, I always think I need the best bass for recording. For my rig, I used an 800RB head with a MESA/Boogie 2x15; I like the way they sound together. I'm not picky when it comes to equipment, but...I've tried a bunch of different stuff, but I haven't found anything else as good."

Regardless of initial or future critical concern or conclusion about the success of 'One Hot Minute,' in the moment of its release, it seemed to fit the band's ever-evolving musical personality, such that, according to bassist Flea, "the album has many different sounds and emotions and feelings going on in it. You really couldn't limit it to just one song. It would be unfair to single out any particular track." For the band, their favorite aspect of the new record seemed to be that it had been made at all, and that they had successfully adjusted to Navarro's playing without having to limit themselves stylistically in the process. Underscoring the aforementioned conclusion, lead singer Anthony Kiedis explained, "my favorite track is different every day. It depends on the mood that I'm in because all of these tracks are very meaningful to me. They were born and grew out of honest experiences, sad experiences, happy experiences. And… those experiences are expressed in these songs."

Navarro to seemed to feel the album was a result of art imitating life, echoing his band mates in explaining, "I think we all relate to each other in our personal experiences whether they be joyous and happy or traumatic and sad and that's what this album is. It's a combination of all our personal experiences thrown into the mix to create a beautiful and wonderful combination."

Critically, the album was very well received. *Rolling Stone Magazine* noted with glowing approval, "*One Hot Minute* is a ferociously eclectic and imaginative disc that also presents the band members as more thoughtful, spiritual—even grown-up. After a 10 plus-year career, they're realizing their potential at last… Now their belief in the power of jamming, innovation and spontaneity is fully unleashed." Though the album would tide fans and critics over, ultimately it was only a temporary fix while the band waited another three years for John Frusciante to return permanently to their musical fold. During the band's hiatus between 1996 and 1998, Flea would briefly join Jane's Addiction alongside Dave Navarro for a reunion tour, and the soundscape of popular rock would undergo a reshaping with the rise of rap-rock's popularity. This would serve as the perfect platform for the Chili Pepper's return in early 1999 with *Californication,* an album that at last had Frusciante back in the fold.

Part VIII
Californication

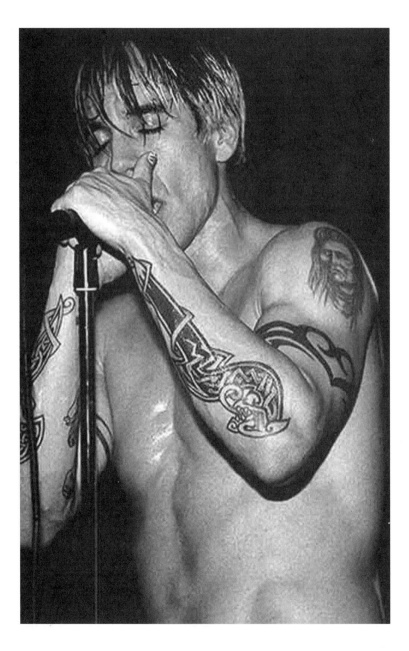

1999

On 1999's disarming and brutally beautiful *Californication*, the Red Hot Chili Peppers nailed the truths of human security and vulnerability to mainstream consciousness in a way that pierced the heart of every listener, whether desired or not. Nothing forced exactly, but rather a loss of virginity that is impossible not to enjoy, but difficult to process at its outset because it quickly becomes overwhelming. Once accepted, its beauty takes breath and gives it again almost subconsciously. The freedom that is taken in with the album's listening experience is so much a rush that the euphoria of sex is the only accurately comparative analogy. The disarming honesty it evokes in the most numbing of moments that only come when we feel naked enough to let ourselves completely surrender to our primal loves and hates. Whether a shelter or an asylum, the core truths of humanity that the album's songs and subject matter explore and analyze are among the most brave to be faced by a rock band—lyrically or musically.

Comparatively speaking, perhaps only a cocaine drip strips away the ability to care about the consequences of honesty the way *Californication* does. It's an innately helpless reflex to embrace the album, and only through such a surrender is the redemption its musical and lyrical sensibilities offer possible. From 'Scar Tissue' to 'The Other Side' to 'Californication,' the album of the same title brought the 1990s back down to reality. Its topical matter was sharp, and it cut deeply into the numb that had previously overtaken rock. Not only that, but it gave listeners new hope, in the Red Hot Chili Peppers as the voice for the outcasts as the hair metal scene started to make a comeback via rap-rock in the late 1990s.

Even though the Chili Peppers had ironically co-founded the genre with Anthrax and Fishbone, they had outgrown that earlier inception with Frusciante's infusion of structure and advanced melodic musicality. In the process, they had redefined the playing field, making room for both the meaning of embracing and the mindlessness of letting go through the sophisticated soundscapes the band routinely created with the guitarist. Riddling rock 'n' roll full of honesty, though the individual members of the band may have gotten sober, the album was their group therapy. It was also a rebirth for them musically and commercially; such that, according to newly re-inducted guitarist John Frusciante, "it was a second chance for all of us. There is a weird chemistry between us. The way I play guitar, it only works when Flea is the bassist, and Flea on can write songs the way he does when Anthony sings. In a way, we're all co-dependant and we know it, but we also trust each other."

The longest road back was clearly Frusciante's, beginning with guitar playing, something the musician admits on the outset of recording *Californication:*

> the only reason that I make music now is because Flea and Anthony had the belief in me that they had when I rejoined the band. Because I'd play with other people around that time, like Perry Farrell, but he couldn't see it as the future. He had no belief in me. He just knew what I was at one time, and what I was now, which was significantly less than what I had been. Whereas Flea and Anthony saw what I could be. They had a vision. I don't even know that they knew what I could be. To them, they just thought I was great right then. They just thought the sound of us playing together is the greatest thing in the world. It's just a chemistry that's there. I don't think they were thinking, 'Oh, in five months he'll be good.' They were thinking, 'This is the greatest thing in the world right now.'…It didn't matter that my fingers were very weak and my guitar playing didn't sound the way it used to

sound, and that I couldn't think as quickly musically...
They didn't see any of that stuff. They saw in me what I
was capable of, and for that I'll always feel indebted to
them.... It's the best thing anybody ever did for me.

That faith on Frusciante's band mates' part was, as Flea explained,
no great leap. He felt closing their eyes and throwing caution into
the musical winds was the way the band had traditionally gotten
their best results with Frusciante anyway, a process the bassist
explained, "jamming...works really well for us...We don't talk
much about songs or how songs should be constructed. We just start
to play and see what happens, how they develop. We improvise a lot.
We find a groove. We experiment and somehow it turns into music.
With Dave, it wasn't possible to work like this. With him it was
more like a long thought process, endless discussions and it took a
long time. We talked about what riff should be played and all that.
With John it's completely different. We just play. I don't mean to
diss Dave in any way. He is a great person and he's a great guitarist,
but the way we work is just different. You never know why it happens with some people and not with others. It's pointless. It's like
asking why you fall in love. There is no real reason, nothing that can
be explained or that would make sense."

Anthony Kiedis explained his feelings on faith: "the most important
thing I've learned...was expect the unexpected. There were times in
my most despondent periods when I couldn't see it getting better. I
was *so* wrong. You can never predict what's going to happen, so
you've just got to keep the faith." Expanding on Flea's sentiment,
drummer Chad Smith reasoned that "with bands that have been
around for 20 or 25 years, you get a kind of musical telepathy...You
can't manufacture that. It can only happen from just doing it—
being connected and wanting to be connected. That's why I love
going to see a band like Cheap Trick or Aerosmith—they're just regular rock bands, where it's been the same guys in the band all along.
Musicians who have been playing together for 20 years or more have
definitely got their own thing." At the urging of producer Rick

Rubin, the bad had embraced Transcendental Meditation. Flea explained "Rick…turned me onto meditation…about four years ago…It helps me to just be in the moment and not be scared of pain and anxiety."

Recalling the circumstances by which the band decided to ask Frusciante back in to their fold, Anthony Kiedis recalled that "when we realized that it wasn't working with Dave anymore, and I think Dave realized that probably around the same time that we did, we just decided to go our separate ways. A few days later I went over to Flea's house to discuss what do we want to do, and he said, 'What do you think about playing with John?' I said, 'That would be a dream come true, but it seems very unlikely.' And he said, 'Well, I don't know, I have a funny feeling about this,' and he called John up. And John having sort of come full circle himself, we just carried right on."

Anthony Kiedis recalled that Frusciante's induction back into the band: "the very first time we all went into Flea's garage studio and plugged in, it was a very beautiful feeling…We just played…I definitely never worried about it or had any doubts or fears, especially from the very first day that we played." Kiedis' decision to just play music rather than discuss why Frusciante had left the band, according to the singer, seemed to be the best strategy to getting over the devastation of John's initial departure from the band: "I was confused and it hurt, because you know, for one thing, John and I had gone from being very best friends…to just being completely alienated from each other. Now seven years later I see that it all made perfect sense and it had to happen that way."

Clearly, the fact that the band wrote, played, and simply fit together musically helped Kiedis realize that the band in fact belonged together. He explained, "chemistry is beautiful and important to any musical endeavor, and it's also impossible to figure out or force it. And the first time we came together with John Frusciante, that kind of elusive and abstract chemistry was there. But then when he left, I realized that it was harder to write songs and feel spiritually connected to art and music as a band. When he came back I felt it again, instantaneously. Also, we're all actually different blood types and we have one represented by each guy in the band."

From another perspective, Kiedis also seemed to be certifying what another mega-rock band before him, Metallica, had experienced with the death of bassist Cliff Burton and the almost impossible task of replacing him before finding Jason Newstead. Hillel Slovack had been the Chili Peppers' Cliff Burton. Perhaps the highest musical and personal compliment Kiedis could have paid Frusciante was acknowledging that in the last ten years, it's certainly the classic lineup. "Having, you know, Hillel Slovak was also an amazing lineup for us, because Flea and Hillel had a certain brand of tele- pathic communication that only happens once in a lifetime. John is kind of the other classic lineup." It was also important for the band to gel together on a personal level. Frusciante explained that "just the feeling of us hanging out was really great and cool in a way that it had never been before…The way we were getting along together as people was the most important element in my being comfortable with being in the band again and knowing that it was gonna work out. We were getting along and speaking to each other."

Anthony Kiedis seemed to concur, adding,

> Flea had more contact with John than anybody else—I ran into him a total of three times during his years out of the band and it was always kinda strained and difficult for us to communicate…John went off to experience what he had to experience, same with me, same with the rest of the people in the band—and as troubling as it could be when it was happening, in the end it was all kind of perfect…it was beautiful. At first I thought, 'Oh God, we're going to have to talk about the past, and that could be uncomfort- able,' but we just looked at each other and realized that none of that really needed to be discussed because we loved each other, so we just said, 'Let's go play.' And from

the second they plugged in it was the perfect fit. And every time we play live, no matter whatever kind of mood I'm in or jetlag or whatever, I'm totally inspired and look forward to just hearing them play…Now that we're together again it makes perfect sense that we all had to go through some difficulties, some learning, some changing. Now we're all very close friends and in love with what we're doing, whereas when John quit the band we weren't so friendly with one another and we had stopped enjoying what we were doing together. Right now it's just so good I can't really bum out on the past or worry about what's gonna happen next.

Being and jamming in the moment allowed the band the creative synergy to focus on beginning to write what would become seventh studio album, *Californication*. With Frusciante back in the musical fold, Flea explained that the latter process felt like a natural extension of the breakthrough the band had made musically with *BloodSugarSexMagic* in understanding their true potential to grow stylistically beyond musical boundaries of any sort, such that "I think the seeds of that shift were sown with *BloodSugar*…And by the time *Californication* came out, we'd strung together some good records. It became obvious that the early records we'd made had influenced a lot of bands that came up. So I guess people's perceptions of us was no longer as these lunatics with socks on their dicks but as guys who were really taking care with writing music and playing the best they could."

As writing and recording got underway, as amazingly skilled and innovative as Frusciante's playing would sound on *Californication*, according to the guitarist,

> I hadn't spent too much time playing guitar over the last few years, so my hands were kind of weak. They didn't really get extremely strong until we had almost finished recording. I had a really strong right wrist right from the start, but that was kind of cool because that was like a lot

of punk rock guitarists—they have incredibly strong right wrists, you know, from doing really fast downstrokes. So that had an effect on my style of guitar playing during the recording. Which was great because I really wanted to approach my guitar playing from a non-musician's stand-point, because that's the kind of guitar playing that never eats itself up, as you sometimes do if you focus too much on the technical aspect. But I worked really hard during the recording of this album. I was playing guitar con-stantly when we were writing it, and when we were record-ing, I would go home and play for five hours after a ten-hour recording session.

Interestingly, the stylistic results of Frusciante's growing back into playing full-time again was, according to Frusciante, a byproduct of the fact that

the whole time we were writing this record, my fingers weren't as strong as they used to be. And now they are. They probably would've been, with the amount I was playing, but I wasn't focusing on the kind of guitar players who had really strong fingers. I was focusing on new wave guitarists and punk guitarists for the style that I wanted to do on this album. People like Matthew Ashman from Bow Wow Wow—who also was on the Adam and the Ants album Dirk Wears White Socks, Ricky Wilson from the B-52s, Bernard Sumner from New Order and Joy Divi-sion, Robert Smith from the Cure, Ian MacKaye and Guy Picciotto from Fugazi, Greg Ginn from Black Flag, Pat Smear from the Germs, the guys in Echo and the Bunny-men, Johnny Ramone, and people who developed guitar styles not from years of playing, but from years of loving music and then all of a sudden getting freed up by realizing there was no 'technique' that was necessary to express something. People who weren't really technically great guitar players, but were great guitar players because they made up original styles that were their own. I've gone through so much inside the last few years that I wanted to approach the guitar, being in this band, from that stand-point. I just thought it would be interesting and fun if I made that the direction of my playing for this album, and that's what I did...I like *Californication,* because I feel like it's the result of all that searching.

Modest as ever, according to the guitarist, "when I hear *Californi-cation*, I hear someone trying to do best they can at that time."

Frusciante's playing again as much as he was upon rejoining the band served as a catalyst to the album's writing process beginning, such that "everything started when I came back in the RHCP, because I had a reason to play guitar constantly. I didn't listen to music for personal pleasure anymore, but to develop and create a style for the album we were recording. I had a purpose again, and as a side effect I found myself writing songs for me. Being with the RHCP has always been good for my creativity." Once that creativity led into preproduction and the proper writing of the album, the guitarist described the band's songwriting process as one in which...

the whole band puts it together, as a group. Sometimes there's a couple of songs, while I just came in with whole song as a guitar part, as an instrumental guitar part, but still everybody else is doing their thing on it, that is what really makes it a song. It's really the style of us all doing it together. A lot of the songs come up from jams, a lot of times, if I come up with something at home or Flea comes up with something at home. It's just in order to inspire the other guys, to come up with something. Because we come up with countless things, that don't ever go anywhere. It's not enough just being a cool guitar part, it's got to be something that everybody is inspired by and that every-body can put an equal part into...Sometimes something starts as a jam between the guitar and the drums, and then Flea will walk in and start playing bass, and it'll eventually turn into a song. We would also record a bunch of things, and Anthony would sort of go through the tapes all the time. He'd play us tapes like a week or a month after we did them and go, 'This groove is great. We should try to make a song around it.' Because we just write tons of stuff, and if Anthony starts dancing around the room and stuff, we feel like it's good. It was hard to make the album as short as it is. We wrote like 30 songs…We just know how to write with each other better now.

Elaborating further, Frusciante explained,

everybody just writes their part, I don't write any of the lyrics, sometimes I write melodies, but definitely on the last album Anthony wrote pretty much all those melodies himself aside from the ones that had something to do with the guitar part…We all write the music together, but only one person writes the lyrics: Anthony…We write the music and then he writes the vocals, basically that's how it works…Some songs come from jams, and some come from parts that someone writes on their own. In my case, I write a million things that I throw away before I stumble upon something that ends up on the record. Certain things are only good at the moment you write them. Others are good for a while, and then lose something. Some ideas keep getting more magical vibrations attached to them—they sound better and better the more everybody hears them. Those are the things that become songs… 'Parallel Universe,' 'Scar Tissue,' 'I Like Dirt,' and 'This Velvet Glove.'…came from jamming…We improvise every day. We have the same sort of freedom and interaction that people had in the '60s when they were playing extended solos, but we don't feature any one soloist. It's much more about parts and rhythms that balance each other out and create something special…In the Chili Peppers a song starts out a five second riff that's cool as a guitar part. Flea will have a little bass line or I'll have a riff you bring it to the band and we all piece it together. It's a slow process. From the moment…it's initiated when we're jamming it could be five or six months before the song is finished… We started in June 1998, but we took some time off for one reason or another. We probably spent a total of four months rehearsing and writing, and then we went into the studio and recorded everything in three weeks…It happened over a period of about eight months or so. But during that eight months three or four were not spent doing it because Flea left for Australia.

Kiedis explained, "It didn't feel like plowing because we spent a lot of time just playing together and writing songs. We practiced from late spring through summer with the idea that when we got into the studio we wanted to know what we were gonna do." Flea fleshed out the band's vibe during preproduction writing-jam sessions as one in which "it was like we had to get it out and boom. We wrote a lot of songs, 30 or 40. It was us in the garage, jamming and hanging out and playing grooves and putting them together until we felt like we had enough songs to go and make a record. It was quick compared to how most rock bands worked and how we have worked. But we did put a lot of time and effort into making them what they are." Drummer Chad Smith recalled, "the songs weren't overworked. We didn't go around and around about them."

One key element that made writing *Californication* such a pure process was an atmosphere, according to singer Anthony Kiedis, in which "I am totally sober, just because it completely stopped working for me. But the good news is music is a built-in lubricant to create itself. Once you start playing, the sort of chemicals and spirits that get released inspire you to become even more creative. John being sober, myself being sober, Flea being… sober, was hugely exciting and influential to our last recording."

Kiedis explained how Frusciante changed the way the band interacted:

> he's blowing my mind. I feel as good as I possibly could about our future. John is a really incredible person, and right now all he cares about is putting good energy into the universe, and the way he does that is through music. So basically he's doing one of three things: he's either playing live, or he's listening and playing along with music, or he's writing music 24/7. Call John at midnight, and he'll be playing along with an Ornette Coleman record. Call him up at two in the afternoon and he'll be working on a couple of songs that will be good for us. Call him up at ten at night, and he's just finished a mystery novel and is going to go listen to an acoustic Jimmy Page solo that he wants to learn. That type of dedication is heavily contagious stuff, and it just makes us want to write more music and make more records and play more shows and just create more beauty for the world. You know, art is a good thing like that. No matter what's happening in the world, there's always room for some more beauty, so we're just kind of along for his cosmic ride right now.

In terms of how some of the album's specific tracks were fleshed from jammed ideas into full-fledged songs, Anthony Kiedis explained that the lyrics for the album's title track address "the act of the world being affected and saturated by the art and the culture being born and raised in California. Traveling around the world, no matter how far I go, I see the affect that California has on the world. It's about that good and bad, beautiful and ugly." As guitarist John Frusciante interpreted it, "*Californication*...is just a word that Anthony came up with, and then wrote lyrics around, each line of the song being a different sort of perspective on the word. Anthony writes in a certain style. It's about California because that's where he lives, but it's about other places in the world, too."

Regarding 'Around the World,' John remembered that "I thought of that guitar part at my house, and I said to everyone, 'You gotta hear this, but I can't play it by myself, or you'll hear one in the wrong place because it has a really deceptive downbeat.' I had Chad keep time on the hi-hat while I played the lick. Everybody dug it, so I just kept playing it over and over until Flea came up with his bass part." The guitarist also recalled that Flea composed the song's bass line in "maybe 15 minutes. Flea is the best bass player in the world. His sense of timing and the way he thinks is so crazy. I mean, the way that bass line goes with my guitar part is amazing. When we play them without the drums, they don't make any sense. But with drums, they really lock in. Our styles compliment each other, and we really love playing together." John remembers his inspiration for the music to 'Get On Top' as blooming out of his "listening to Public Enemy one morning, and I came up with that rhythm on the way to rehearsal—just tapping it out with my foot. In fact, that's me working Flea's wah pedal with that rhythm at the end of the song."

Once the band formally entered the studio to begin proper recording, the transition was a seamless one. Kiedis explained, "when we got into the studio it was a fluid continuation of what we'd been doing…There was a sense of excitement that we never lost. I don't think any of us ever dropped the emotional love for what we were doing, even though we took time off. I think we always had our eye on the fact that this was gonna culminate in the studio…To me, we started working on this record just a little over a year ago, so to me this record took about a year to write, rehearse, arrange, and record."

Guitarist John Frusciante described his preference regarding the recording formats and routines: "analog sounds the best to me, and I feel that's how my music should be recorded. I'm not gonna go on a big tirade against computers, because a lot of music I really love is done on them. I would point out, though, that somehow, as convenient as computers make things, albums take longer to record now than they did in the '50s or the '70s. So I don't know if the convenience is actually convenient; I think it's just the illusion of convenience, and in actuality it makes things more complicated. You have to work with it, and it brings the best out of you. Magnetic tape is the way I like doing it; it's really fun for me. I like doing first takes, I don't like doing multiple takes, I don't like comping, I don't like doing all that bullshit. For me, the first take has a special excitement to it."

According to the guitarist, the band's preference for tracking live mimicked their habit of writing while they jammed. Frusciante explained,

> it's the interaction; it's the way we write songs. We each play a part that's separate, we don't have one guy just come in and write the song and tell the other guy what they should play. I mean, sometimes you write a guitar part and there's a drum beat that's in your mind that goes with it, and there's no separating them; you can't help it. Sometimes, the drummer you're playing with can sense what that beat is by hearing the guitar part; sometimes you have to tell them the drumbeat. But, basically we have four separate parts in the band that all interweave together to make the song. And if one guys not playing, then the other guys

groove is gonna fall into the wrong sockets. Everybody's gotta push and lay back in the right places to fit everybody's part in smoothly. Everybody's gotta listen to the other guy's part. It's not like the Beatles, where you have a guy write chord changes and the vocals, and then you can record things to follow the other one. Any one part in the mind of the listener can be the main part, and the other parts can be just as prominent, too, if you listen to them.

I try to approach every section differently. Flea and I hit our instruments in different ways for each section, and that creates varied dynamics...In a jam for one song... Flea was just playing the bass line, I forget how it happened, we were just jamming, and I guess he was practicing playing with a pick, and I figured I'd mute the strings like Ian MacKaye does in Fugazi. Then I figured it'd be cool if played a harmony to what Flea was doing. I remember I just started ending it differently: I had the minor 3rd in it, then I had the 4th, and then, when I did the major 3rd, it inspired Flea to do that descending part to resolve it. It was just playing off of each other and just thinking it would be cool to do a harmony with him, with the rhythm and texture like that. It was an important thing to us to make every section have a new texture, like the way electronic music is, where you have each section be all different shapes and different textures. We do that on this album with our instruments...It took us writing and playing together for a while to get to the point where it would feel like that. But when we recorded it it definitely felt that way. We were just finished with it before we knew it... *BloodSugar* we did just as quickly.

According to the guitarist, while the band didn't "record anything with a click track," drummer Chad Smith recalled that "we also found out that we work a lot better if we know what we want before we enter the studio. It took us only three weeks to record the album."

Describing the gear he utilized in tracking *Californication*, John Frusciante explained that

> on this album, I used a real old '65 Marshall. I also used a 200-watt bass head that I used on *BloodSugar*, I use a bass head and a guitar head at the same time; that's how I play. I had a good sound for this album, but Louie—the band's right-hand man—doesn't want me to take the heads on tour because he thinks they'll break. As far as guitars, I used a '66 Jaguar on 'Around the World,' one of the guitar parts on 'This Velvet Glove,' and the odd guitar part here and there. I used a '56 Stratocaster for most of the basic tracks, and a '62 Stratocaster, the sunburst one, on some stuff. I also used this '55 Gretsch White Falcon, it's the kind of guitar that Matthew Ashman used in Bow Wow Wow and Malcom used to use in AC/DC, or *Californication* and 'Otherside' I have .012-gauge strings on it. I'd like to go more into that, developing a guitar style using thick strings like that. It's fun. I also had a '61 Gibson SG, and I used a Telecaster on some things too, like 'Easily' and 'Scar Tissue,' filmmaker Vincent Gallo helped me find a lot of those guitars that are old, collectors' kinds of pieces. He knows more about guitars than anybody who lives in Los Angeles... I play in response to the kind of instrument that I'm using. I play differently on different guitars.

> on the album *Californication,* I mostly play a Fender Stratocaster from 1956, or '55 or something. It has a maple neck and it's really a great guitar. Actually, when I bought it, a guitar expert that was with me insisted that the pickups were original, and the people in the store thought they were original, but after I had finished recording the album I took it to the guy who re-frets my guitars and he said that it had Seymour Duncan's in it that had been made to look like they were the original pickups. But the guitar sounded great, and that's what I used for most of the

basics. There are a couple of songs where I used a white Falcon from 1955, which had .12 gauge strings on it. Usually I use .10s, but this guitar has .12s on it. There's this guy, Ricky Wilson, who was the guitarist for the B-52's. He was one of my favorite guitarist, although he's dead now, but he uses really thick strings and he only used four strings—the D- and G-strings were removed. so he would make up these guitar parts that would go in two directions at once, which was a real cool style and was very inspirational to me. So anyway, I bought this kind of guitar because it is the coolest looking guitar I've ever seen, and I'm gradually coming up with a style on it that fits in with the way Flea plays. I used in on the song 'Californication' and also 'The Otherside.' But definitely the best way for me to play my best with Flea is with a guitar with .10s on it, but it's fun to try to come up with a style that has as much movement and draws colors in just as a colorful way with a guitar with .12s on it. It's very different, 'cause you can't do vibrato as much as on a guitar with .10s, but it's fun. when you get .12s or higher, it starts to sound like surf music, you know, Dick Dale and so on. The notes don't ring out at all...11s are cool—in fact that's what I have on this guitar I'm holding right now which is a Fender Mustang that I bought for practicing in my room. I don't use all that many effects. I use a Fuzz Tone, and a distortion pedal, a wah wah pedal, and a chorus pedal. On stage I can get a lot of different sounds just with those four things. Mostly, I play with a clean tone; it's rare that I turn on the distortion pedal—that's only if I'm going to do a solo, and solo-ing is not that important a part of my style. The more important part is playing texturally and playing different colors.

The producer who helped to flesh out those colors musically, as usual, was Rick Rubin, who, according to John Frusciante, was

> the perfect producer for us…He's not exactly involved in the writing, but he plays a big part in the construction of the songs. He'll tell us if a song needs a section or a part, and he helps us balance the songs so we don't have sections that are too long or too short…We've found that for us we need a producer to be like pretty much devote a few months to us. That's what Rick Rubin does when he works with us, if he's doing something else it stops at least a couple weeks before we go into the studio. We need to feel we've got somebody's undivided attention…He doesn't do any disciplining but that we do ourselves. I love making music and I love writing music and nobody needs to push me to do that. But Rick has a real mellow type of a vibe that he generates when he listens to our music. We know that that's the only thing going on in the world for him when it's happening. He's not the kind of person that gets distracted or comes to the rehearsal studio with something else on his mind or carrying his personal life into the studio. He's very focused and not a big party guy, he's a real focused centered person. And that's why he's the perfect person for us because we can trust him that way. No matter how off center any of us are we know that he's got a clear head about every thing.

Continuing with his praise for the producer, the guitarist revealed,

> I love having him as our producer because he says very little to me, as far as the guitar playing goes. I just do what I do. He helps the arrangements of the songs. He comes to the rehearsals, and he's just a great person who knows whether or not things are good. We recorded this record at a regular studio—Studio Two at Ocean Way Recordings in Los Angeles, but we did it on the same kind of board

that we did *BloodSugar* on. We were just so excited about recording music; we recorded the basics in a week and a half or so…We talk about things after I've already done them, in my case. I mean he did the whole time, when we did the basic tracks, he mostly focuses on drums and vocals. And as far as my backing vocals, he usually, when I do my backing vocals I might do them over the whole song and then he says 'Wanted you take them out at this part?' or 'Wanna you do something at this part?' So we talk about it afterwards and then I do some things more or take some things away based on what he says…The harmony vocals weren't even my idea, but Rick Rubin's. He led me there, at first even against my will.

Addressing some of the specifics of how different guitars and effects were utilized in recording various tracks on *Californication*, guitarist John Frusciante recalled a wide variety of gear, including using

a '55 Gretsch White Falcon…on 'Other Side'…through the Showman and a Marshall 4x12 cabinet. For the break-down section, I used a '61 Gibson SG Custom into a cranked Marshall JCM 800. I think that's the best kind of distortion—a humbucker into a Marshall, like Eddie Van Halen…On 'Scar Tissue,'…that was my '55 Strat with the maple neck—most of the basic tracks were recorded with that guitar. I think I ran it through the Showman because the Marshall wasn't clean enough…I used that technique— taking two notes that are far apart and playing them in a cool rhythm—on my first solo record. 'Scar Tissue' is a very simple example of the technique, but I think it's a style that sounds like me…I used a '65 Telecaster for the slide parts in the song…There are two different solos—I just turned on a fuzz pedal for the second one…There's some nice slide playing on 'Scar Tissue.' I just played the slide on a Telecaster into my Fender Showman amp. My favorite slide guitarist is Snake Finger. His influence isn't evident on that song, but that's how I practice slide: from playing along with him and Jimmy Page…I'm doing it in standard tuning because I'm just doing single notes. If you're trying to learn Robert Johnson songs and stuff where it's a lot of chords, you need a different tuning. But when you're just soloing, I don't see the reason for changing the tuning. It doesn't really matter how it's tuned…

For 'Get on Top,' I used…the Ibanez WH-10. They don't make them anymore, but it's the only wah I use. Other wah pedals are very wrong for me…Other wahs seem to cut the volume in half and the tone isn't as thick—it's suddenly smaller. With the Ibanez, the tone stays big, and it has a really wide range. It also has a switch for either bass or guitar. For 'Get on Top,' I used the bass setting. The solo on 'I Like Dirt' was played with the guitar setting…I used the '55 Strat. It's the best feeling neck ever. I'm going to gig with this one and the '62 with the rosewood neck… In rehearsal, I was playing more screaming guitar solos for this song, but I ended up playing that solo with a '56 Gibson ES-175 that had .013s on it. I didn't use the 175 for too many things—only 'Porcelain' and this solo…I was thinking about Steve Howe's solo at the end of Yes' 'Siberian Khatru.' The band sound is really big—and they're playing fast—and then this clean guitar comes out over the top. It's really beautiful, like it's on its own sort of shelf. For 'Get on Top' I wanted to play something that would create a contrast between the solo and the background… On 'Savior,' that heavy delay tone is my '55 Strat into an Electro-Harmonix Micro Synth and a 16 Second Delay. Even though it's a weird sound, it's inspired directly by Eric Clapton's playing in Cream. If you listen to the actual notes, they're like a Clapton solo—they just don't sound like it because of the effects. I don't think anybody's guitar playing is better than what he did in Cream. I don't think there's any reason for a guitar soloist to try to go anywhere beyond that. It's the ultimate. It's possible to create other musical colors, of course, but as far as solos go, I think that's it.

We had a song on it called 'Phat Dance' that had a backwards guitar solo on it. It's not on the record, though. That song will come out, but the vocal is gonna be changed slightly. Anthony was real bummed about that. But I do plenty of backwards guitar on *Niandra LaDes*, if that's what people want to hear. I would've liked to have that solo that I did on 'Phat Dance' be on this record, but I went into that so deeply on *Niandra LaDes*, I don't really feel like it's something I have to do…When I'm playing backwards, along with the chord changes, I just follow the chord changes. Every chord change that I'm following, it doesn't matter if I stumble going into it because that's just gonna be the end of the chord when you hear it forward. Those notes that I finally found are gonna be the first ones you hear, so it's always gonna sound like it goes right along with the chord. You get a flow going, and you just play to where it sounds good and has a form backwards, and it'll have another kind of form when people hear it forward.

Of all Frusciante's playing on *Californication*, two of singer Anthony Kiedis' favorite pieces of the guitarist's work are "'Road Trippin,' and 'This Velvet Glove.'…They mean a lot to me, because John plays two guitar parts; it's one of the few songs that has an acoustic rhythm track happening. That's important, because I'm a terrible guitar player and could never play that part."

Upon completion and release, *Californication* would sell 13 million albums worldwide, and re-invent the Chili Peppers' fan base to include an entirely new generation of fans. According to *Rolling Stone Magazine,* the band had

settled down and written a whole album's worth of tunes that tickle the ear, romance the booty, swell the heart, moisten the tear ducts and dilate the third eye. All this inside of song forms and production that reveal sublime new facets upon each hearing…The real star turn on this disc, though, is by Anthony Kiedis, whose vocal cords have apparently been down to some crossroads and over the rehab, and returned with heretofore unheard-of range, body, pitch, soulfulness and melodic sensibility…proves once again why he's the only ax slinger God ever wanted to be a Pepper, too. As in days of yore, Frusciante continually hits the mark with slithery chicken licks, ingenious power chording, *Axis: Bold as Love* grace notes and sublimely syncopated noises that allow the nimble Flea to freely bounce back and forth between bombastic lead and architectonic rhythm parts on the bass. If there were a Most Valuable Bass Player award given out in rock, Flea could have laid claim to that bitch ten years running…While all previous Chili Peppers projects have been highly spirited, *Californication* dares to be spiritual and epiphanal, proposing that these evolved RHCP furthermuckers are now moving toward funk's real Holy Grail: that salty marriage of esoteric mythology and insatiable musicality that salvages souls, binds communities and heals the sick.

The album's writing and recording had certainly seemed to heal the band, and reveling in its success, lead singer Anthony Kiedis pondered upon its successful release, "who would have thought that *Californication*, 18 years into our career as a rock band, would have been our biggest album…With this album we had so much stuff. We never felt we were hitting writer's block or feeling the pressure in any way. Nobody talked about sales and there's nobody punching cards when it comes to working. We do it all in our own time."

Flea concurred: "the truth is…only once have we made two records in a row with the same lineup, and that was *Mothers Milk* and *BloodSugarSexMagik*. We liked *Mothers Milk* at the time, but *BloodSugar* was leaps and bounds beyond it. I don't know if it's going to happen again, but we just made *Californication* and we just think that it is the greatest thing that we have ever done… This is our greatest and best album, thank you."

Finally, the album had helped guitarist John Frusciante rediscover his personal and musical soul and center: "I look at myself in the mirror, and I see myself as being somebody smaller. I think the fact that I'm that kind of person brings a certain element to the group. Anthony was destined to be the superstar, and Flea was destined to be the entertainer. But I think my destiny was to be an more introverted guitar-player and songwriter who has learnt how to entertain." The band seemed finally at peace, and based off the success of *Californication*, they would enter the millennium as one of the most critically respected and musically and culturally relevant bands of the day.

Part IX
By the Way

2002

Rolling Stone Magazine best articulated the Red Hot Chili Peppers' musical evolution in their review of the band's eighth studio album, *By the Way*:

it turns out *Californication* was only foreplay. With the accomplished, insanely melodic *By the Way*, the Red Hot Chili Peppers dive headfirst into the pop realm that their 1999 single 'Scar Tissue' hinted at. They swim around in the same inviting Southern California waters that inspired the Beach Boys, and discover that the incandescent hook can say as much as, if not more than, the testosterone-driven backbeat. A near-perfect balance of gutter grime and high-art aspiration, the Rick Rubin-produced *By the Way* continues the Peppers' slow-motion makeover…Slyly, without doing anything drastic to alienate their core audience, the Peppers have shed their early devices—the jerky raps, the faux-P-Funk rhythms—that were once innovative but quickly became the stock tools of every rap-metal hybrid in the land. Along the way, the Peppers' songs got more intricate, acquiring string riffs and heroic guitar counterlines, and pretty soon this band of loutish love thugs became the alt-rock Aerosmith—minus the screeching-and-beseeching power ballads, creators of music that could be at once credible and commercial. The transition has been so gradual that those who were on the scene in the rowdy 80s followed right along and stayed as the band made its lunge toward art. On *By the Way*, these reformed groove savants head out on an even more radical pursuit, chasing that elusive moment of giddy, unspeakable bliss most often found in the work of Brian Wilson and the Beatles. They don't only want to reference that kind of writing, though—they work to take the songs there.

Continuing, the magazine commented that

singer Anthony Kiedis' utopian love themes and hot-oil sex scenes have been raised to a *Pet Sounds* level of refinement. The hooks, most from the pen of guitarist and budding auteur John Frusciante, are sweet but never syrupy. The Peppers have never been this consistent: even the seemingly mindless songs come with consciousness-expanding bridges instead of just salacious vamps, and they toss out sprawling existential questions—'Is it safe inside your head?' as often as they strive for tidy answers. *By the Way* would be notable just for its parade of relentlessly catchy melodies…But here is where the band's years spent perfecting the deep-funk groove have paid off: Even the few obligatory mawkish ballads are delivered as though they were urgent bulletins from some metaphysical front line, with an intensity rarely heard on multi-tracked recordings. Anyone can build a song around a simple command such as 'Throw Away Your Television'; the Chili Peppers take that idea, lash it to a romping beat that recalls the Ellington orchestra's 1930s-vintage jungle jumps, and turn it into something positively galvanizing, the seed of a get-off-the-couch revolution. Similarly unexpected references turn up throughout *By the Way*—Kiedis stretches his voice into some Beatlesque psychedelia…It's one thing to mix things up until the pedigrees are obliterated. It's another to do what the Chili Peppers have done: gather disconnected sounds and ideas from all over the map into something that's cohesive and bold, and, despite its mongrel origins, couldn't come from anyone else.

In other words, the Red Hot Chili Peppers were on their own musical level, a plateau no other rock band had ever reached. Not just rising to the occasion, the band had traveled beyond all expectations with *By the Way,* elevating rock 'n' roll to a new level at that point in the early millennium. With digital downloading in full swing, rock fans needed an extra incentive to go out and actually spend money on a CD when they could just as easily sit at home on their computer and steal it for free. With all that *By the Way* offered fans, it would have been disrespectful not to go out and spend the money as the band had definitely given fans a bang for their buck.

According to Rick Rubin, a key to the musical doors that had been opened on the album was "John being back which makes a huge difference…He's brimming with ideas, and he lives and breathes music more than anyone I've ever seen in my life." Anthony Kiedis also "really outdid himself" lyrically speaking, and it sounded as if—according to the singer—he was attempting to become more emotionally extraverted, such that "I've never felt comfortable writing 'love songs' or 'relationship songs,' but it's sneaking in there and certainly not in a typical way…When I read through my lyrics I can see where she's kind of the initial point of inspiration…I put less sexual aggression into the songs and try to give them more soul. I don't feel like I have to hide behind an image anymore. I am who I am. I'm not a sex machine. I'm human, a spiritual being and there is nothing wrong with showing emotions. Things change and people change. Now, I see being able to be emotional not as a weakness. I see it as strength. Even my lyrics are far more personal and, of course, due to that, more emotional…In very obscure, less than obvious ways, I feel a lot of it is about either being in love or the desire to be in love. It's definitely what I've been feeling for the last year. A profound sense of wanting love in my daily experience."

Musically speaking, the collaboration between Kiedis and Frusciante in writing *By the Way*, as Kiedis recalled it, began with

> John and I getting…together in his room at the Chateau Marmont, where he was living at the time…and we worked on some more obscure pieces together. Like the song 'Cabron,' which sounded almost like he'd written it to be a flamenco guitar instrumental. I just loved it because there was energy in there like crazy. I took home a rough copy of it from a low-tech tape recorder and started thinking of vocal lines to go with this music. John and I are both very much in love with doo-wop—vocal music from the 50s. I was feeling that kind of energy, but with a Mexican flavor, 'cause the soul of Los Angeles is largely fueled by our Mexican population here. So I started singing kind of a doo-wop melody to this really wild acoustic guitar instrumental. I brought that into the band, and it took Chad and Flea awhile to find their places in it—because it was so different and weird for us, coming from left field.

Elaborating on the influence of harmony-heavy derivative music on the duo's writing, Frusciante explained that "I remember Anthony coming over during one of the first songs we were writing, and I asked him, 'What do you think about backing vocals being a bigger part of the album this time?'…So, when we'd be working on a song, I'd be listening for a part that would be good to have a backing vocal. I was really inspired by a lot of doo-wop music from the '50s and a lot of '60s pop music and Queen."

As always, lyrics remained the sole territory of Kiedis, and on *By the Way*, he was topically a world-traveler, covering everything from commentary on his own home-town of L.A.—a Chili Peppers staple—to musings on the divine. Kiedis, in addressing the former, explained that *By the Way* was about "a night in the life…It's a landscape of L.A.—an evening that happens simultaneously across the entire city, and the feeling of anticipation and hope and joy of going out into the fray. Maybe you're going to meet some magical adventure partner that's going to warm the cockles of your soul and sing you songs and hold your hand and take you to places to go dancing. But it's also about people getting beat up, and drug deals happening, and prostitution going on, and car crashes and people playing dice. It's about all of this stuff happening at the same time."

In addressing divinity, Kiedis cited the spiritual 'Don't Forget Me,' which the singer identified lyrically as "a cornerstone of our record, because no one's ever heard us play anything like this… This song is my ideal of what God is, and what life is, and what this whole picture's all about, and how it's just everything and everywhere, and the good and bad and the in between, and the experiences of a lifetime… I think it will be our opening song for the next three years or so because it puts us in such a good mood."

Diving into a description of the musical side of writing *By the Way*, Kiedis cited the album's title track as a summary example of the rainbow of colors the album explores musically: "*By the Way* encompasses a lot of different aspects of the record and a lot of different aspects of the Red Hot Chili Peppers over the years, and sums it up in one bombastic, yet melodic number that feels really good to play…Even though there seem to be more accessible songs we could have chosen for the first single, we chose to go for something more raucous and colorful."

With the band fully recovered from the process of adjusting to John Frusciante being back in the band, the guitarist seemed to be more musically sure of himself in terms of guiding the flow of the musical derivatives that influenced the album's musical direction, explaining that, during its writing, "I was definitely in this kind of place, where I was the center of things. The feeling of that probably didn't stop the whole time, that we did *By The Way*. At the moment now in this new badger stuff, that we recorded in the last month it's felt much more like a band. While doing *By the Way* it often felt like I was doing stuff by myself."

Still, Frusciante seemed to find no pressure in the role, perhaps viewing it as an opportunity to build on the comeback he'd made with *Californication*, explaining that "like *Californication*, writing *By the Way* has been one of the happiest times in my life. It's been a chance to just keep on writing better songs and improving my guitar playing... The time when I was working on new songs for the band every day was the best time in my life. My only reason for being here is to wake up in the morning, listen to music and play along on my guitar to songs by which I want to be influenced. If I happen to get ideas, I grab my tape recorder. That's what makes me happy...I wanted this album to have more dimension, more different sounds and more movements in the chord progressions...But I also wanted it to be more fun."

Frusciante described the amazingly creative process by which song ideas first originate for him:

> there's a certain feeling that runs through my brain, through the music I listen to and through my life. I knew that feeling was going to be the essence of my music, and that certain people were going to gravitate toward it. I can't take credit for the feeling—it's something that's been there since I was a little kid. I never had any doubt that I was going to succeed. Most importantly, I knew that I was making music for the right reasons. Music is not something that you are in control of. It comes from somewhere else. If you're that middleman between the cosmos and the real world on earth that the music comes through, you are very lucky. When you record music, it's not your job to try to control anything. It's more about being in the right place and flowing with the energies that are in the air around you and with the people that you are making the music with. The second that someone thinks music comes from themselves, and that they are the ones responsible for it, is when they go off track. The most important thing you could realize is that you are the least important part of

the whole process. Music is going to be made whether any one artist is here or not. If John Lennon or Jimi Hendrix had disappeared, music still would have gone on, changed, grown, and been the beautiful thing that it is. You take away the music, all you have are the individuals, and they don't mean anything. The individual is nothing—it's the music that's in the air all the time that's important, and you have to be humble in the face of that…If the song wants to come to me, I'm always ready to receive it, but I don't work at it. I always did it since I was a kid, so I learned very well to recognize when it's time to write and when I'm imposing it on myself.

Continuing, the guitarist explained, "if I get an idea that's just an interesting guitar part, and I have no vocal idea for it, then that's always for the Chili Peppers…I feel like when a song is written, the whole thing has already existed prior to the first idea in the song coming into this dimension…The shapes and the colors and a snapshot existed of it in a dimension that had no time. To me, giving it that form and then presenting it to people makes the place that they're from grow and become bigger." Once an idea has entered his mind, the guitarist explains that he typically prefers to write on either acoustic guitar or "sometimes I write on an unamplified electric guitar. I have a few old Martin's, two small-bodied O-15's and an O-18, at my house that date from the 40s. I usually write songs on one of those. And I always bring a couple of acoustic guitars on the road with me to write with. Writing songs on an un-amplified electric has its drawbacks. The guitar is so quiet that I sometimes sing in a high falsetto voice that doesn't really work when I do the final recording. So I've learned to write on the acoustic and actually sing in the style that I want to use on the final recording."

Frusciante's ever-evolving derivative influences for his playing styles on *By the Way*, which always depended on what music he was listening to personally in that time, included an eclectic mix:

People like Jimmy Page and Jimi Hendrix have pretty much been my gods the whole time I was playing. I also like Eddie Van Halen's early guitar playing. But I don't feel like guitar playing went any further after that—not in that technical or flashy direction. And I don't feel like guitar players have started coming at it from a new angle. So I began drawing inspiration from synthesizer players—programmed music, starting with Kraftwerk. It's another way of approaching melodies that guitar players don't really do. For the whole time we were touring for Californication, I was practicing guitar by playing along with electronic music...I did have a few guitarists who I was intent of emulating and who were big influences on my sound on By The Way...Like Vini Reilly from the Durutti Column... The main thing about his guitar playing is that it's really textural. There's lots of really interesting chords and shapes and you can't really tell what's going on. It's a combination of his Les Paul plus some echo, flanger, chorus and phaser and not using distortion. You can't tell what you're hearing...I have to really sit down and listen carefully to find out what's going on. He's just a great guitar player, full stop. I wanted to listen to these people who weren't just about technique but more about textures. People like Johnny Marr, John McGeoch from Magazine, Siouxsie and the Banshees, and Andy Partridge from XTC. People who used good chords.

Beyond guitar players, Frusciante detailed some of the album's other instrumental writing influences:

I learned all Gary Numan's synthesizer parts on the guitar because that was very much in the way that I wanted my guitar playing to be. I was spending a lot of time learning parts from Kraftwerk and Depeche Mode, Human League and Orchestral Manoeuvres in the Dark, because I was finding that people who were programming synthesizers in this early electronic music were playing in a very minimal way, where every single note means something new and every note builds on what the last notes were doing...I was thinking of writing chords that are dense—that have more to them than just a root, third and fifth. These chords have 9ths and 11ths and 13ths. I tried to make the guitar pretty impossible to figure out correctly. I learned a lot throughout the making of this album from studying Charles Mingus and learning his chord progressions. I studied a lot of music books, and learned about the way different people, like the Beatles and Burt Bacharach, construct chord progressions—just things that I would never have been able to figure out by ear. It started changing the way that I play guitar. Johnny Marr of the Smiths, Electronic was also a big inspiration in getting me to think about the guitar differently...John McGeoch. He's the kind of guitarist I want to be. He has a new and brilliant idea for every song. I usually play along the stuff he is doing in the Magazines' albums and Siouxsie & the Banshees' 'Juju.' I was listening a lot to the Sparks' albums *Propaganda* and *Kimono in My House*. Adrian Fisher is the name of the guitarist, but I'm sure it's Ron Mael, the songwriter of Sparks, who tells him what to play. I was listening to Johnny Marr from The Smiths and Vini Reilly from The Durutti Column, the way they kind of weave a pattern with the chords. Keith Levine from PIL was an influence on the song 'This Is the Place.' In the way my tones bleed into each other.

Elaborating on the latter, Frusciante further explained

I think that in each era period of time there are the same energies, which make it possible to create good music. But all of this is a question of being impartial in such sense that you see that those energies take on different shapes in different periods of time. For me those energies that once

made Jimi Hendrix create new sounds are the same energies that come over Depeche Mode when they recorded
Violator—an album that does sound like no other rock
album before. Well, you know, there was a time in my life
when I was a little child and I thought: Music was at it's
best in the 60s. But I don't feel this way anymore. The
more I opened myself to all varieties of electronic music of
the past 20 years the more I had to realize that some of this
stuff is at least a guiding and exciting as the music before
it…When I grew up I was only thinking about technique.
I had a goal: no one, absolutely no one, could disagree
with me being a fantastic guitarist. My way of succeeding
was to learn from people who were generally considered
impressive: Eddie van Halen, Yngwie Malmsteen…But I
surrendered that thought. It didn't fit the band's music,
and it lacked originality.

The guitarist continued,

I began following the colours in my head and I didn't care
about how many tones I could play in the smallest amount
of time, or how fast I could move my fingers up and down
the fret board…Keith Richards doesn't care about technique
in that sense: if he'd done that, he would never have played
the brilliant guitar solo on '*Sympathy for the Devil*'… That's
how I practice. Melodically, I'm far more influenced by
Kraftwerk records than by guitarists' solos… During that
period I was very interested in learning about chords and
understanding chord theory better-the application of 9ths,
11ths, 13ths and all of that. And it's really much better to
practice that sort of thing on an acoustic guitar, because the
richness of harmonics is so much deeper than with an electric—the way the notes of a chord resonate together. Amazing things happen on the acoustic guitar. Sometimes you
find chords were you can actually hear notes that you're not
playing, because the combination of harmonics ends up

resulting in an additional note. You might be playing a six-note chord and you can hear a seventh note. You can hum that note. You can point it out to other people and they can hear it too."

Discussing the expansion of taking his own song ideas and incorporating them into a band dynamic by writing music with Flea, Frusciante explained, "sometimes I bring the entire guitar parts for a song along and the others add their parts we did this for example with 'Venice Queen,' 'Cabron,' or 'I Could Die For You'. Things such as duration or arrangement are of course developed by all of us together. 'This is the Place' and 'Don't Forget Me' are jam session songs and do sound like the sessions during which they came around. During those jams Flea played the same bass line for over half an hour and I tried various guitar parts on top of it. Flea loves it to put himself into a hypnotic groove. I join in and as soon as he has caught me I will play one part after the other each one giving Flea's bass line a completely different flavor. Those songs don't sound like the bass is playing the same part all the time, but he does."

Frusciante continued,

> when your bass guitarist plays something very hard, very fast and you are joining in also playing hard and fast, then this will not trigger any special feeling in your head. But if you play something simple and spacious, you will see that a feeling develops, a feeling that is totally different from what happened when listening to the bass line for the first time. Maybe it's this way of putting things side by side, this kind of harmony that I mean when I speak of colours. If you look at a collage by Max Ernst you will find different textures next to each other. These aspects can be transferred to music. Things like a perspective where you can see something clearly in the background and where the foreground is blurry. In music this means that things don't have to be straight all the time to make sense and to work

out. The individual elements can be completely different from each other and yet they can harmonize.

Frusciante claims that he Flea are so tuned in musically to one another, that they often flesh out songs together by thinking in one another's instrumental terms—a step in the process that the guitarist believes "is very important when you are playing with someone. If the other has an idea, you shouldn't just add something that is like this idea. You have to play something opposed to what the other does. I guess that Flea and I have an advantage that whatever we play works out quite well. Even if I try to disagree with him musically things blend in perfectly and disagreeing makes it then even more colorful."

Another aspect of achieving the latter came in a collaboration specifically between Frusciante and producer Rick Rubin. The duo worked on were orchestral parts based around colorful vocal harmonies, such that, according to the guitarist, "Rick Rubin and I would get together every day, and he's got these CDs of AM radio hits from the 60s. And they'd have stuff by the The Mamas And The Papas and songs like 'Cherish' by the Association and 'Georgie Girl' by The Seekers. All those songs are all about harmonies. I've been practicing harmonizing a lot in the past year and a half. My friend Josh and I would sit around and sing Beatles songs, or that Velvet Underground song, 'Jesus,' which has a harmony in it. Anything we could think of that had harmony."

Producer Rick Rubin further explained the point of the process:

> I think for a band that's been making albums for a long time…finding new ways to express themselves keeps it interesting. And on this album there were lots of lush vocals and an orchestra, which we'd never used before, and that just took it a new way. Maybe the next album will be much more sparse. I don't know the direction it will go, but I know that evolution and change is a good thing… Flea has got simpler and Flea has got more interested in

following chord patterns and swirling around with in chord context. He's got more adapted working around with chord changes and things like that, which is a really skillful thing to do. I find a lot more to be interested in the kind of bass playing he does on *By the Way* or *Californication* than I do in what he was doing on *BloodSugarSexMagik* or especially *Mother's Milk*. To me what he does now is more interesting, like on the last record there was kind of attention between us, that made it to there. We weren't really hangin' out together and coming up with this idea and that idea back to back. It was more like me in the studio by myself just doing whatever I could think off to do to the songs."

Continuing, Rubin recalled,

the music that we recorded recently in the last month, where we were in the studio and recorded 17 tracks, he was more integrated into the process and we were both coming up with ideas back to back, both trying things out. It was kind of more like the thing of anything goes, if somebody in the band has the idea. To me that makes more good vibes on the record. There are those of us, who actually love listening to records that have that vibes going on the making of it. I'm definitely one of those people, but as far as being in the band myself it's a much much more pleasurable experience of listening and of recording when there is no resentments or real unspoken feelings going on between any of the members. So I really enjoyed going back to the band. I liked the sound of something like *BloodSugarSexMagik*, which is what we have going on right now on this new stuff. And we are probably doing another writing session, where we write some more songs. We definitely will and I hope that band feeling continues to there, because it's something, that makes our new stuff very enduring to me.

Once writing was complete, Frusciante described the process by which the band fleshed the songs out fully as one in which everybody sought to up their game: "I think that the two most beautiful moments in my life were the recording sessions for *Blood-SugarSexMagik* and *Californication*. That's why I'm really looking forward to recording again." Chad Smith validated Frusciante's role as musical, explaining "John really inspired us to take it to the next level on this album...On *Californication* he had just rejoined us, and he started writing music right away. But we hadn't really had time to reconnect, personally and musically, through touring, traveling together and spending time back at home. The chemistry of our band is so important. And now John is a really key, integral part of this new music that we have."

Anthony Kiedis echoed Chad Smith's sentiments, noting "John is always deeply disciplined and committed to living and breathing his music at all hours of the day and night. That's pretty infectious." Musically, *By the Way* highlighted the Red Hot Chili Peppers' ability to musically re-invent themselves over the course of every new album without losing touch with their core musical foundations, a goal that seemed important to Frusciante throughout, with the guitarist reasoning that "bands start being lame when they start repeating themselves and try to determine what was great about their past glories and then try to relive them... With us, we're just trying to make new music that we find exciting and that we like to play, and to do that, it has to be new and exciting and good-sounding to us...I feel that there is still more territory to cover musically. I feel like we're getting better. I see Flea growing as a musician; I see Anthony growing as a singer and songwriter. I feel like there's a lot more to do within the context of this group that is of interest to me... It's good for a band to be together, be on the same plane. That's why for *Californication* and *By the Way* I had a lot of a happier experience than when I'd worked on *Mother's Milk* or *BloodSugarSexMagik*. There's a lot less bad energies around now we're all coming from the same place."

As involved as Frusciante was at the musical helm in writing *By the Way*, he clearly and selflessly felt that "I know what Anthony and Chad and Flea have said but I think of it more as a band effort. I do put a lot of energy into everything, sure, but I don't underestimate that the real energy comes from the four of us... That's a sound that's made by four equal parts that blend together to create an identity. The way we write is completely democratic and selfless. It's no single vision...That's number one over any of our individual efforts...Now each of us appreciates the other. In the BSSM era everyone believed he was the most important member of the band, while now we are aware that individually we don't count. We know it's important to create together. We think the world is what others make, not what we make singularly."

As a result of the band members all being in the same personal and creative headspace, according to the guitarist, the creative result was "much deeper, I would say, than the last record...There's a lot going on...on some songs. When it's the right thing, it's just the four of us playing...There was just all kinds of new rhythms and new sounds and nobody really sounded anything like themselves. We weren't playing the way we play on *Californication*. The energy, the whole energy was even more so whatever the energy on *Californication* is. It was that energy multiplied. That alone makes me really excited about the next record because we just have a completely new sound just because we've all given a lot of thought to music in the last year-and-a-half and we've gotten really tight."

Frusciante shared more of his own musical observations on how his band mates had risen to the challenge and occasion in context of tracking the album—which as always the band did live:

> Flea was playing with a pick. He's been learning Peter Hook's Joy Division-era bass lines. And I've been playing in a different sort of way that's been influenced by this electronic music that I listen to. I'm approaching the guitar from a completely different headspace...Chad was

playing really interesting beats. Some of it was really heavy and it felt really good. How do you describe these things, they are feelings I know the feeling of our next album very clearly in my head. I know that there are a lot of new rhythms and new sounds for people to hear. Everything we do it's going to be fresh…When we made *By the Way,* Anthony Kiedis and I discussed me doing a ton of harmonies all over the album. We were gonna make my voice be an equal element to the music as the guitar, bass, or anything else. This is something that Anthony was and is still very in favor of. I wasn't actually listening to the Beach Boys until the last couple of songs that I did. It was toward the very end of the album that I went into an obsessive period about the Beach Boys. While I was making the record, it was more the Beatles, Erasure, Queen…All the vocal melodies on this new album are Anthony's own. Sometimes they were suggested by the guitar, or whatever. But in the past there was more interaction between me and him as far as changing the vocal melodies around. And on this album I didn't really do that. I would think more about what I was going to do with the harmonies.

Prior to the beginning of the album, guitarist John Frusciante explained,"we rehearsed for a few days before the South American shows…we were jamming and coming up with ideas for new songs. It was great and I love the new sound so much…It's the freshest stuff we've ever done." Once the band had entered the studio, Rick Rubin became the group's silent fifth member. Frusciante recalled "Rick is so incorporated into what we do in the band that it's hard to pinpoint exactly what he does, but he definitely infiltrates…In the Chili Peppers I definitely contribute production-type ideas, but a lot of things end up being compromised. I might record a ton of different sounds and things like that for a song, but Rick is always going to favor the lead vocal in the mix…I mean he's as much a part of the record as any of us. It's just in a more ethereal, kind of feminine way. You can't say, 'Oh, there's Rick.' Brian Eno produced records where you can tell he treated the guitar, so you know it's an Eno-produced record. There's nothing like that with Rick, but he's all over the record just in terms of his ideas. The fact that the record is as concise as it is has a lot to do with Rick."

Explaining the live feel of the album the band wanted to achieve, guitarist John Frusciante explained their preference "to use click tracks as little as possible. Sometimes Rick suggests it, and we'll do it just to feel what it would be like to play exactly in time. But we never like the way it sounds when something's recorded with a click, and usually switch it off when we go for a take." The band tracked most of the album live off the floor, but, as the guitarist explains, in certain instances, "we were doing it separately, like I would be in one place, doing my backing vocals, and Anthony would be in another place, doing his lead vocals. But guitar overdubs, I do them." Once the band had finished principle tracking, "we recorded 28 songs in the end, some of which will be B-sides, 14 made the final cut. There was definitely a lot of good stuff, but we didn't have time to work on everything we wrote."

Regarding the equipment that influenced the writing of specific cuts from *By the Way*, on the track 'Cabron,' Flea explains that he used a Hofner Bass with a capo on it, because "John suggested it...That song was a little frustrating for me; it took me awhile to find the right bass line. Basically, I had a bass line that I loved, but everyone else didn't like it. Then John said 'Use a capo, it'll make it sound completely different.'" Elaborating, Frusciante recalled, "on the song 'Cabron,' the acoustic guitar is capoed. I really love having the capo. I've been learning a lot of Johnny Marr things recently, and it seems like he always used a capo. There's also a lot of capoed acoustic guitar on the Jethro Tull album Aqualung, which I was listening to before I wrote '*Cabron*.'" On the tracks 'Throw Away the Television' and 'Don't Forget Me,' guitarist explained, "I'm playing 16th notes on a DigiTech digital delay... but the echo is set to where it's doing triplets. That whole song, by the way, is played on only the high E- and B-strings."

Frusciante explains that the riff for 'Can't Stop' was inspired by "Ricky Wilson, the B-52's guitarist. He died around 1985, one of my heroes. He took off the D- and G- strings and tuned the upper strings to the same note. He considered the low and the high strings as two separate things and often played them simultaneously into two opposite directions. It's a simple way for him to give the impression of using two guitars. This is exactly what I tried on 'Can't Stop.' The high notes move back and forth while the lower ones change chords." Regarding the inspiration behind 'Oh Mercury,' Flea explained that "we'd…always listen to ska, but we never, ever had a ska sound on one of our records…But John came in with this great guitar part, and we just did it. It had a natural, free-flowing feeling that just worked." Frusciante added that "I was listening to a lot of ska and reggae at the time, but I didn't think of it being a ska groove when I wrote it…But everyone called it that. I think what made it more ska in my eyes was when Flea played the melodica."

Addressing the guitar sound he was aiming for on *By the Way*, John Frusciante explained:

> for *By the Way* I deliberately looked for a not-Jimmy Page sound. I listen to music and guitarists so different that in my style there is a bit of everything. That's why I play in a way that doesn't resemble anyone else…That's how I play guitar. I consider it important to always think of the space between notes when playing. I regard silence and music to be completely equal. When you play a note you change the silence that was there before you played the note. One always takes silence for granted, but one really has to see how it is changed through playing. So why not integrate silence into your musical concept from the start? It is really exciting to look at music from this point of view…but I also did some artistic games in my mind with music. I

understood that often good things to listen to are those that combine the tough and the soft, kind sounds with rough ones, sometimes they mix soft and rough, kind and tough also. Antirealistic combinations. Most of the people wouldn't dare to do that. If the band has a strong sound and the guitarist plays in a delicate way, it sounds freaky. But this is what I used to do then, and I still do now. The only difference is that they like it too now, because they know I don't hate them. So if they play hard, I play soft. If they play fast with small and short notes, I extend them and make them flow. In that way we get an artistic balance.

Frusciante elaborated:

the way I played when I made *By the Way* with the Chili Peppers, where I tried to make the songs harmonically unique by using interesting chords. At the time, I was studying Charles Mingus and the Beatles—anything I could get my hands on that relied on abnormal chords. I learned a lot from that, and I still use unusual chords here and there, but I've regained an excitement for what you can do with just an Am, Dm, a D, and a C. Sometimes it takes just living your life a certain way to be able to open yourself to the rhythm of the cosmos, to the point where you can use those familiar chords in the same way you might speak a few simple words of love to someone. A few of the most basic words in the language might be the most meaningful thing someone can hear, and the same can be said with basic chords...Also, there are no blood 'n' guts guitar solos. There is nothing of the guitar-hero kind of thing. I don't show off for the sake of showing off. I'm not after drawing attention to myself. I subordinate myself to the song, in order to raise the song forward. On every song I have a new idea of color and sound. It becomes more like melodies, instead of traditional solos.

Another new element to Frusciante's guitar work on the album was the presence of reverb, which the guitarist explained he'd "never really done before…That's one of the main differences in the guitar sound. I was really influenced by all the surf music I've been listening to. I had an old Fender spring reverb. Toward the end of the project, for a couple of overdubs, I started using the Holy Grail digital reverb pedal by Electro-Harmonix…I was playing a lot bigger, denser chords than just your standard triads or whatever, and I wanted all those intervals to come through clearly. I'm not really into distortion except for solos, feedback and stuff. There were a couple of times when I used a Gibson SG straight into a Marshall, which is the best kind of distortion. My favorite guitarist is Bernard Summer of Joy Division, and that's what he uses."

Elaborating further on the specific gear Frusciante utilized in capturing the guitar sounds he achieved on *By the Way*, he cites a 1962 Fender Stratocaster with a rosewood neck which the guitarist explains he used because "that '58 Strat has a bit of a cleaner sound, and it always seemed to sound better for what I wanted on *Californication*, but for this album, the '62 just sounded right straight away—it sustains better—so I stuck with that pretty much all the way, apart from and SG on a couple of songs… Regarding micing, I always mic guitars with Sure SM57…Whenever someone tries to put a Neumann on my amp, it just ruins it for me."

Utilizing various Taylor acoustic guitars throughout the album, Frusciante's amplifier rig included a 200-watt Marshall Major and a 100-watt Marshall Super Bass, one of which he usually ran in a stereo set-up with a Blackface Fender Showman guitar amp pushing the Marshall. Additionally, he uses the Ibanez WH10 wah-wah pedal, which the guitar player explained he kept

> in a trebly position…Additionally, I was using a lot of effects. We wanted to create a real sense of atmosphere. I used a few Line 6 echo pedals, an Electro-Harmonix flanger and the Big Muff a lot…As far as amps, I was using

this big Fender spring reverb from the 60s…I used it with a modulation synthesizer—that's the sound you hear on the "Throw Away Your Television" chorus. As you'd expect by the name, it has 'great reverb' but also a really thick sound and a great tone. I listen to a lot of surf compilations, and there's a lot of really cool surf music that came out of the early 60s that was made by 15 year old kids and that's how they sounded…On 'Don't Forget Me,' I used and envelope filter and I was using the volume pedal a lot on that song too—and that Line 6 pedal in one of the analogue delay settings to where it's constantly feeding back. Just as it was about to feed back, I'd just turn the knob as I'm playing to prevent it from going into full-on feedback. It gives it that spooky kind of feeling.

Flea, for his part, recorded playing a Modulus bass with a Galien Krueger head on a Mesa/Boogie Amp Cabinet

On the scope of his responsibility within the studio, the guitarist explained, "you do need a lot of energy for the recording process, but actually it goes boomboom. We go in, record the songs, I do my overdubs and ready. Okay, meanwhile I have the additional assignment, singing backing vocals. I must wait on Anthony's singing lines, until it's my turn… When we made *By the Way,* I'd never recorded harmonies in a studio by my own will. Rick had forced me to do backing vocals for *Californication*, which at the time I wasn't into. It wasn't until Guy Picciotto of Fugazi was so complimentary about my harmonies that it made me think, 'Oh, wow—harmonies. Great!' Before that, I was like, 'Harmonies suck.'" As bassist Flea recalled, Frusciante also introduced keyboards into *By the Way*: "John did a lot of things we hadn't done before on previous records, like synthesizers and keyboard parts… It brought a whole new color and feeling to the record that hasn't been there before."

Frusciante really thought that the keyboards would enhance the album's musical textures: "I think a big reason for that is that a lot of elements on *By the Way* are mixed very soft. I did all kinds of little synthesizer things that are barely audible. A lot of the time my guitar is barely audible. The mix is definitely done in a really subtle way. When you have a lot of things that are just barely at the level of audibility, you tend to feel them more than hear them, and that creates a sort of ethereal quality... Late at night after Rick leaves...I like treating other instruments and things like that with my synthesizer, that's always late at night. I love the way of working relationship that we have. He is really, like coming in and makes everybody feeling comfortable and he just lets things be when they're fine. He doesn't have any striving for perfection, he understands that little imperfections are sometimes what makes something being great and colorful." Another area where Frusciante took on new additional responsibility in the studio came in the album's post-production mixing stage. The guitar player recalled, "I was very present for the mix of *By The Way*. It was the first time I was in a production of this importance—a huge responsibility for a novice...poor Rick Rubin!"

Upon completion, the band seemed elatedly excited with the creative results of their labor, satisfied it had achieved their goals, which among others, according to Flea, had been to expand on what he felt had

> always been a real femininity to our music…But I guess it's not heard so much when something is really loud, distorted and jammy. To me the biggest difference on *By the Way*—apart from the fact that it's more layered than any of our records—is that it's less jammy. There are more songs and less solos and jamming out. There's definitely improvisation going on within the structure of the song. But the structure is much more…structured… Both individually and as a band, we are growing and changing and finding new ways to express ourselves. This is definitely a different record for us because our lives are different, because we are different people every day and are always writing and changing and arriving in different places. I'm very proud of my playing on this record, but I'm also proud of being a part of something that is in touch with the energy around it. You know, in our communal compositions on the record, something is moving and changing, so for me to be selfish or say that I got notoriety for being this fancy, fast, funky bass player would be silly, and it wouldn't be relevant to me. When I play songs that we wrote 10 years ago, I respect them for what they are; I honor them and pour my heart and my body into every note—but for me to not change and grow with it would be stale and uninteresting.

John Frusciante also commented on the stylistic and derivative comparisons; the album "reminded me of the early Public Image. I was playing a textural wall of sound and an influence of dub music in some of it. Really spacious…This is the freshest stuff we've ever done." Responding to the question of whether record sales ever figure into the band's barometer for whether an album's creation was a creative success or not, Flea explained, "we don't feel pressure like that, but we might feel pressure sometimes from having to work a lot every day…Having to follow something creatively isn't a pressure for us. It's a challenge. We just get in there and do the best we can."

In terms of whether he felt they had, in fact, done their best, Anthony Kiedis mused that "I can't even tell if it's good anymore…I mean, there are days I feel like this is the greatest thing we've ever done, and there are days that I'm like, 'This is just going to die in the water.'" Not surprisingly, the album didn't die in the water, it stayed afloat the Billboard Top 200 Album for months, selling four million units, and ushering the Chili Peppers into the new millennium of rock 'n' roll as one if its most commercially iconic, musically significant, and brilliantly vibrant stars.

Part X
Stadium Arcadium

2006

John Frusciante always referenced Jimi Hendrix derivatively in his playing, but on *Stadium Arcadium*, the guitarist becomes his millennium equivalent. This latest installment required two CDs to fit all of the new musical frontiers and innovations. The ninth studio album by rock 'n' roll's most commercially-durable free spirits was sure to be another multi-platinum hit. Very much the sum of its individually brilliant parts, the band's 2006 studio album, *Stadium Arcadium,* was a constellation of four stars all shining as brightly as one another. Musical and rhythmic orgasms woven with melodic harmonies and soft, silky string and acoustic instrumentation, the record is by far the band's most diverse and complete musical achievement, encompassing 28 songs. *Rolling Stone Magazine* hailed the record as "the most ambitious work of the band's twenty-three-year career—an attempt to consolidate everything that is Chili Peppers, from their earlier, funnier funk-metal stuff to soul-baring 'Under the Bridge'-style balladry to Californicating vocal-harmony pop. And unlike…almost every other double album of the post-vinyl era, the band pulls it off."

Ironically, according to Anthony Kiedis, despite the record's wealth of material, originally

> we wanted to do quite the opposite…Our plan was to do a short, sweet, simple record. Something that was easily digestible…We just ended up writing enough songs for about three records…So making a double record just seemed to fit. It's funny because making this one has been a lot less taxing than our past records have been. The workload was a lot

more intense because we wrote so many songs and recorded them all. But we are getting along better, everyone was happy and confident, and when you hear the new songs, you can hear that everybody's hearts are in them all…I think we always go into writing…with this mindset that this time, we're going to write the perfect 11 songs and just put out 11 songs like they used to do in the days of Buddy Holly and the Beatles…Those early records were so short and sweet, and had this kind of lasting profound impact on the world because they're very memorable and digestible and, I don't know, maybe it just takes less energy or effort to connect with smaller collections. But as has been the case with every single time we've tried to do that, we end up with 30 some-odd songs. The difference this time was we ended up liking all of those songs and finishing all of those songs and it actually became a very difficult process to even just whittle it down to 25.

Guitarist John Frusciante recalled that "usually we record 25 songs, Anthony records vocals on 20, and we end up releasing 15. This time, we finished 38 songs! At this point, I even consider that keeping 'only' 25 in a double album constitutes a regression, proportionally speaking. I battled for a double with 30 songs! When you write music that you judge satisfying, you want to transmit it to a maximum of people, it's human. Every song of this album deserves to be transmitted to the public. God didn't give us music for the only selfish pleasure of those who write and play it." According to the singer, the band began preproduction "every day we showed up to this funky room in the Valley where we write music, and everyone felt more comfortable than ever bringing in their ideas…Everybody was in a good mood. There was very little tension, very little anxiety, very little weirdness going on."

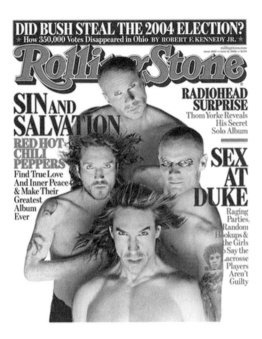

Remarking on the progress the band had made personally and professionally since their first album as a foursome back some 16 years earlier, Kiedis reflected that "there had been so much water under the bridge between then and now…We were in a state of growth and change and desire and enthusiasm in 1990…and then we went through all of these different times and episodes and hardships and joys, and then we kind of came back together and found ourselves as a band, as songwriters, as friends and figured out how to be better co-workers…So we were a little better at it when we came back. It wasn't quite as confusing, and we didn't have the same types of demons going through us as the first time we came here…It was a…more loving experience this time around."

Anthony Kiedis also described the process of writing lyrics and vocal harmonies: "they don't make it easy for me…They could be an amazing jazz-fusion trio. But somehow I find songs…in the bigness of what they're doing. It's not like I get to decide: 'I want this.' It's this unspoken moment of consideration, where as a unit we listen to these parts and meditate on what serves the song best…It's all the weird little fun stuff that you think about when you take a walk... This incredible girl I met, or this really bad feeling I had about myself that everyone else seems to have about themselves—an endless amount of things that may flow through your mind when you're open to it, and you just start turning it into songs. When I listen to my band play, and just be spontaneous people with music, it really just triggers ideas and thoughts and melodies and lyrics, and all I have to do is listen to them."

Elaborating on the band's songwriting process, drummer Chad Smith explained, "we always feel pretty creative as far as writing songs. We write them together; we just get in a room, or on occasion in Flea's garage. We just sort of improvise, like jazz musicians. It's very sort of spontaneous and organic, not a preconceived sort of jamming. Now we record everything, 'cause sometimes you'll forget, you know, 'What was that thing again?' So we record everything. Sometimes one of us will have a riff or a bass line from home but it really gels when we come together. We really have a strong special chemistry that we take advantage of when we get together."

Guitarist John Frusciante further expanded...

> as songwriters, for us the challenge is to find new ways of peaking other than the obvious ways...We started to record the album a year and a half ago and during that time we've been listening to the album for like 14 hours every day. Since we finished it, I haven't listened to it again. I think it's the best album we've done until this date, the more psychedelic, the darker, the deepest if you want, and the most eclectic. Sometimes when you pick up the best songs to be part of the album, just by chance they all sound in the same wave, let it be funky, rock, fast or slow, but in this album we've tried to pick up the songs from a wilder range. Personally, I wanted to do songs that sounded harder, but at the same time, that they would transmit something deeper, more transcendental. The separation between funky songs and melodic songs started with '*BloodSugar*'...*Stadium Arcadium*

is the first time we mix these two elements in the same song, or at least is the major perfection grade we've achieved. On the other hand, I also wanted that every guitar solo was an event for itself. Not in the meaning of display myself or being a virtuous with the strings. I mean using the experience of all these years and just know where I should play simple but effective and where I should go straight to the rhythm and the groove of a song to raise to the maximum its potential.

Continuing, Frusciante explained,

> while we were doing the album I listened to guitar players like Clapton, Hendrix, or Jeff Beck, and on the other hand artists who are not famous by their solos, like Siouxsie and the Banshees or The Smiths. When we rehearse, we just start playing and when we come up with a melody or a solo that we like we just look at each other and by then we know we have something there… I don't want to give myself limits. I learned to play again by coming back in the band. At the time of *Californication*, my fingers were still weak. I asserted my technique with *By The Way*. And now, I push it as far as possible: I want my playing to be powerful, twisted, ambitious, and chaotic. I want it to explode in all the directions. Reject the idea of playing clean and straight, encourage the tortuous, the bad, playing before the rhythm after the rhythm, sometimes even ON the rhythm. The most beautiful way to sing liberty is to let instruments express themselves together. Flea, Chad, and I needed to challenge each other: everybody wanted to bring the other on their field, to play with him, to show that things don't have to be quiet and cute to be organized: chaos can be a form of organization; from hitch can be born synchronization.

Offering additional insight into the band's songwriting process for the album, producer Rick Rubin explained that one of the band members might "create one main element, a verse or a chorus, and from that find pieces to make other parts of the song. Most bands write a lot of riffs, then see how they fit together to make a song. The Chili Peppers are more organic: creating pieces to go with other existing pieces…Once the foundation of a song is built, John takes the song over the top…It's not a lot of experimentation. John has the idea. And if he goes too far in any direction, the other members pull him back in."

Guitarist John Frusciante elaborated on Rubin's aid as a producer: "he doesn't do any disciplining but that we do ourselves. I love making music and I love writing music and nobody needs to push me to do that. But Rick has a real mellow type of a vibe that he generates when he listens to our music. We know that that's the only thing going on in the world for him when it's happening. He's not the kind of person that gets distracted or comes to the rehearsal studio with something else on his mind or carrying his personal life into the studio. He's very focused and not a big party guy, he's a real focused, centered person. And that's why he's the perfect person for us because we can trust him that way. No matter how off center any of us are we know that he's got a clear head about every thing."

Echoing Frusciante's sentiments, singer Anthony Kiedis remarked that "he really has earned his place as the producer of this band… He has improved his game consistently. He just gets better and better. He's willing to work harder and harder. His intuition flourishes. We have been so willing to grow and change as a band, and he's also come along for that ride. He has the same love for music today that I think teenagers get when they're 17 and they fall in love with the wonderful world of music."

Amazingly, while Rubin maintained control of the console during recording, Frusciante had adapted his now-extensive knowledge of the recording process to an extreme "where I learnt how to use the studio like an instrument. Up until that point, I was still letting the engineer tell me what to do. On my solo albums, I worked with my friend Ryan Hewitt who is a young engineer ready to experiment.

We began a relationship where, starting with *The Will to Death* we decided to everything differently to seeing how it was done around us. By the time I was doing my overdubs for this record with Ryan, we just had it 'down'. On this album we actually had 72 tracks, because we had to have a 24-track machine for the basic tracks a 24-track machine for overdubs and treatments and another 24 for backing vocals so when we were mixed there were three 24-tack machines all sync'd up with each other. I needed my solo albums to be able to get to this point. Now, when I'm in the studio, I'm in control of what's going on. The engineer asks me what to use."

According to producer Rick Rubin, the band's pace was more measured this time in spite of the massive expanse of material to be covered during recording sessions:

> they decided to work shorter hours…In the past, the writing mode would be a very exhaustive process and they would be in there for a long period of time and it'd be tiring. In this version, they worked less days a week but carried it on as long as it took. And they took a lot of breaks. So there was much more of a freshness—there was never the drudgery of showing up on the 100th day and trying to energize. Just naturally, as an experiment, they decided to see what this felt like, and by cutting down their hours, they ended up being much, much, much more productive…Recording-wise, it went very quickly… There was a very fluid momentum. Everyone always plays at the same time, but typically the instruments are really isolated from each other for control over the sounds later. John thought it would be an interesting concept for this album for all the instruments to be in the room at the same time, so all the instruments are bleeding into each other, and that was the first time we had done that.

Elaborating on the band's studio etiquette, engineer Ryan Hewitt recalled that "they're pros, and they're incredibly talented…They rehearse their stuff, they look at each other, they lock in, and they just go for it, and Rick really pushes for that. He wants a natural, organic feel, and so does the band. They don't play to a click track. Everything was done on tape. There's no ProTools involved. What you hear from the band is exactly what they played, when they played it. There's no trickery involved in the music on this record. It all came out of the fingers and hands of these guys."

Perhaps to maintain the same karmic vibe that had inspired and guided the recording of *BloodSugarSexMagik* 15 years earlier, the band moved into the same haunted Laurel Canyon mansion to record, with singer Anthony Kiedis explaining that "we had some new spirit to work on…We had new feelings, new emotions, new songs—it was a different time for the band. We were in a different psychological state the second time around than we were the first time around. We were looking to go to a warm and inviting place."

Guitarist John Frusciante elaborated, "it just seemed like the perfect idea because I live about one minute away and Anthony and Chad live about 10 minutes away. Flea's about an hour away in Malaga, but because of the way it's set up, he could sleep at the studio. Flea made it his home for the weekends so it was just practical in that way. Also the studio we normally use, Cello Studios closed down… It was a lot different now than it was back then. The feeling was a lot warmer, a lot cozier. A certain amount of work had been done on it: there were some nice carpets, and a parachute had been put up in the tracking room as a ceiling hanging. When we did *BloodSugar*, it was just a big empty house when we brought in some equipment and started tracking. This time they had a couch in the tracking room. Little things like that. It didn't seem as devoid of life as it did the first time."

Frusciante described their technical set-up as one in which…

> we recorded to three synchronized 2-inch, 24-track machines, running at 30ips, and mixed to analog tape as well…The board was a Neve 8068 with 31102 mic preamps, and that Neve 1057 and 1073 mic preamps were also used for some tracks…The basic tracks, including most solos, were cut

'live' in the studio, with everyone playing together in the same room. For a lot of it we even had our amps in the same room with the drums, and we allowed for bleed, as I was really into trying to capture some of the atmosphere of '60s recordings, and also have that extra push you get when you know you've got to nail the take because you're all in the same room... We had one 24-track machine for the basic tracks, another 24-track for overdubs, which were mostly guitars, and a third 24-track for the vocals. There was a lot of tape manipulation of the guitar tracks as well—varispeeding the tape to put the guitars in different octaves, or flipping the tape over for backward effects. For example, on the solo for *Stadium Arcadium*, I flipped the tape over and processed the guitar through an old EMT 250 digital reverb that was then run through a high pass filter from my modular rig. So it's backward reverb, filtered. I did three different passes of that, listening to the track backward and opening up the high-pass filter on the reverb. Then I flipped the tape over and took the best bits of the three passes—did a comp, basically—and then erased what I didn't need. I did the same thing at the very end of 'Come On Girl,' where Anthony comes in singing and there's a guitar that answers him. The filtered reverb sound turns into the real guitar sound. If you tail it right, that's the sound it produces, as if sounds are coming out of thin air.

To capture the album's guitar sounds, Frusciante explained a mic set-up that included "a Shure SM57 positioned on axis a couple of inches from the cone. On some tracks the engineer, Ryan Hewitt, added a Royer R-121 ribbon mic, positioned about 15 feet away, in order to capture some of the room sound. We used a Telefunken Ela M 250 tube condenser mic on the acoustic guitars." Elaborating on some of the gear he brought into the studio for guitar tracking, Frusciante recalled that "I bought a bunch of different wah pedals because there were so many moments on the album that were going to have wah-wah that we didn't want them all to be the same. My favorite one is still the Ibanez WH-10 one…The Dimebag model was another one I used on certain spots on the album. I don't like it as much as the Ibanez, but it's the best that I've found…Sometimes I'm experimenting with the modular synthesizer, and sometimes I hear the sound clear in my head so I know exactly what I'm setting out to do. Some effects are impossible to control, like the new MuRF pedal by Mooger Fooger. It's basically a series of 10 filters that go in a rhythm, and you can turn up each frequency at any moment. I used that on the solo at the top of the verse on 'Dani California,' and I also used it on Flea's trumpet on 'Death of a Martian."

Continuing, Frusciante explained,

> on this album, I used the same guitars and amps I've always used: My sunburst '62 Strat and white '61 Strat go into a Boss Chorus Ensemble, and the stereo output on that splits out to my 200-watt Marshall Major and Marshall Silver Jubilee. I also have a '69 Les Paul that I put through just the Silver Jubilee with one cabinet. But after the guitars went down to tape, I'd process them through my modular synth gear. A lot of people might think they're hearing effects or even a keyboard synthesizer, but that's not what I was using. There are parts of a synthesizer that make sound, and parts of a synthesizer that process sound. And I was using only the parts that process sound, like filters, low-frequency oscillators, and envelope generators… For effects, I did use the new POG Polyphonic Octave Generator from Electro-Harmonix, which is what's making the guitar sound just like an organ on 'She Looks to Me' and 'Snow.' I used the new Electro-Harmonix English Muff'n, too, which is a really cool tube-driven distortion box. And, of course, I always use a Big Muff and a Boss distortion pedal and my Ibanez WH-10 wah.

Describing his tireless process of research heading into any—and specifically this—album's recording, Frusciante fleshed out his strategy for going after a more 'free-wheeling' sound in that he didn't want any of his solos to be rehearsed, in spite of the fact that

> when we were rehearsing for this album, I was probably listening and practicing with my guitar for about five, six, seven hours a day. A lot of music for this album came from me just playing and playing. A lot of what I was listening to was hip-hop, so I was playing bass along with it and then I would pick up my guitar and play for an hour and see what came out. I have the patience to play the same thing over and over on my guitar until something new comes into it from meditating. A lot of my time was also spent memorizing long Jimi Hendrix Solos… Another part of my concept for this album was to make it more raw and to let certain mistakes fly. If you listen to 'Especially in Michigan,' I had my guitar on the wrong pickup. I like the way that riff sounds on the bass pickup, but when I was playing the song I looked down and it was on the wrong pickup. You can hear it when Anthony starts singing: there's a little commotion going on where I stop playing the riff or a second and you hear the sound change, then a little white noise for a second. I'm happy to leave it like that because it gives the recording personality. That's the kind of shit they would leave in during the 1960s but take out in the 1980s. Which time period was better? The Rolling Stones' recordings in the 1960s had the tambourines and drums going off on different times with each other; the guitars go off time with each other then come back together and it's beautiful. That's what gives it personality and a magical feeling. I am a perfectionist, but for me those kind of accidents are perfection.

Elaborating more in-depthly, the guitarist recalled

> I'd been listening to a lot of hip-hop and R&B, where people are doing a lot of free rhythmic expression over the music, ignoring the strict 16th-note grid that musicians

tend to play within all the time. I started noticing that singers and rappers like Andre 3000, Ermine and the people in Wu-Tang Clan were finding their own polyrhythmic relationship to the groove. Plus, I grew up studying Frank Zappa's music and the polyrhythms that he used. So I started getting into this idea of things being off time and yet in time. I was also listening to a lot of music that had a blues vibe to it, and when I started putting all of this together at rehearsal, the result was a lot like Jimi Hendrix, because he was playing with that same off-time rhythm thing a lot. That led me to study his playing, which I hadn't done in a few years. I started seeing it in a completely different way once I began specifically analyzing his rhythmic approach... I'd begun studying Hendrix again, I was playing along with his hits. I'd learned them as a teenager, but now I had a new approach to them...For the guitar solos on *BloodSugarSexMagik* and *Californication*, I knew what I was going to do more or less in advance...or at least I knew how I was going to start and end them. I wasn't going out on a limb too often. On this album, almost every solo happened spontaneously. I had no idea where I was going to start or end, and that's also due to this rhythmic approach I've discovered.

Expanding even further on the conceptual and derivative influences that informed and impacted his playing on the album, Frusciante explained, "for this album I tried to keep the passion and the atmosphere that old teachers transferred then but using techniques they didn't use back then. It's not about moving forward, but it's about moving to the sides and explore other ways. I partially agree with people who I respect, like Bjork, when they say we have to totally get rid of guitars, because I'm not satisfied either with what it's being done with guitars these days. But on the other hand, I'm a guitarist, I can't help it, and it's a challenge to me to do something unusual or new...You have to break rules to keep forward, and I'm afraid most of the guitarists these days just follow the rules with no risk...For

Californication and *By the Way*, I was focusing on music from the 80s…Whereas on this album I was after what people like the Jeff Beck Group, Led Zeppelin, Cream, Black Sabbath and Deep Purple achieved in the late 60s and early 70s. All those groups were doing something that was able to bring pleasure to a large amount of people, and at the same time they were breaking new ground and doing something deep. At that time, it was just natural for groups to do that."

Delving into an explanation of the philosophy behind his playing stylistically on the record, Frusciante revealed:

> my reasoning is to take that kind of playing guitar from the 60s and 70s and to use it in a context of songs coming from a new place, a place that is mishmash of all the influences I got from the music of the 80s and 90s. I fit it to a new environment, by using a sound those guys didn't have at that time. For example, I learnt a lot from the techniques of production of people as George Clinton and Brian Eno. In the early 80s, Eno treated guitars and the other instruments with new synthesizers. Today, I make things with my guitar. My state of mind is to say 'What would Clapton have done with Cream if he had had a modular synthesizer?' I try to think in that perspective: 'Let's try to make an interesting thing, in a sound point of view, but with a range of sounds they didn't have in the 60s.'… Now I'm really into using synthesizer gear…like a big guitar effect—using the guitar signal, rather than oscillators, as the sound source. I'm inspired a lot by what Jimi Hendrix was doing with his guitar on Electric Ladyland, or what George Clinton was doing to Eddie Hazel's guitar, or what Brian Eno was doing to Robert Fripp's guitar. These were people who didn't want sound to just sit there; they wanted to hear some kind of movement going on all the time. That idea was very important for me on this album. In some ways I went further than I ever though I could go, and in some ways I didn't go as far as I would have liked.

Engineer Andy Hewitt noted,

> John had an instinct to leave imperfections in a record…
> He's a huge fan of 1960s, 1970s music, where there's just
> stuff that's blatantly wrong on certain records. It's not per-
> fect. John recognizes when to let go of things. There are
> other times when we'll sit there trying to fix one note for-
> ever until it is perfect. But there are some things that are,
> to me, really obvious—Chad dropped a stick in one song,
> and that was left in. You can tell because he's playing kind
> of weird. He's trying to find his other stick, but it keeps
> going, and he's playing with one arm. It's things you don't
> notice when listening to the song because it was so good
> and the groove is so tight. If you listen to the guitar by
> itself, it might sound a little funny in one spot. But
> because the band is so tight, that kind of thing is not going
> to stick out, and it will add to the cool factor.

Touching specifically on the ever-presence of guitars, which thickly
layer the album, singer Anthony Kiedis explained,

> John has got over his 'less is more' phase and has unleashed
> his guitar beast within! So it's a little bit more guitar
> aggressive…He's totally on some higher uber-Beethoven-
> meets-Hendrix-type shit…Sonically, it's quite rich and
> deeper in layer and texture than out past recordings, which
> has a lot to do with the guitar…John's always had an
> understated confidence…But he likes being loud now,
> and part of that came from hanging out with the Mars
> Volta…Being at the forefront, going for the heavy blistering
> guitar in your face: John's always been capable of that. But he
> didn't feel it. Now he feels it…There's this ongoing progres-
> sion of everything else that has been slowly happening
> between *Californication* and *By the Way*, with harmonies and
> textures. John has really fallen in love with the art of treating
> sounds. The album's layered, but not in a heavy-handed way.
> John's work is definitely of the masterpiece quality, as a

guitar player and sound treatment-ist. He has certainly gone to some weird über-level of hearing some Beethoven-sized symphony shit in his head. He really shines on this record.

Fleshing out the differences between his playing on past albums and this one, Frusciante explained that

> back then I didn't do many overdubs. *BloodSugar* was naked. At the time that was the concept I wanted…The template for *Stadium Arcadium* was to have an album like Black Sabbath's *aster Of Reality*where the guitars are in stereo, hard left, hard right, and it's just the simple power chord and sounds so thick as you'd ever want it to sound… Almost every solo was improvised. Even those that sound like they have been written were improvised. The solo in Wet Sand for example, is one of those ones you can sing along with but it was totally improvised. What's the key to improvisation? In polyrhythmic playing, when you're finding your own groove inside the music, you can't plan out what you're going to do. Take the guitar solo to 'Hey,' I could only plan it out in the sense that I knew I was going to be constantly speeding up and slowing down. If you try to plan the subtlest difference in the groove of drums and bass is going to change what you are doing. During the rehearsal we were playing stuff much faster than we ended up playing in the studio, so the same solos weren't really working. So I really had no choice but to wing it in the studio. For me, this really gave the album a live quality and an exiting spontaneity that I haven't had in the studio before. There is no more relaxing part of making a record than improvising solos. That's just fun for me.

Flea rounded out the band's focus on heavy guitar rock in the course of recording their latest album by explaining, "John often puts limits on himself as a guitarist…He wants to make a stylistic statement, so he doesn't just let go and play. But on this album, he did both of those things. But there are also times when he just let fly with a Hendrixian, Pagian flurry of loudness."

Delving into some of the individual songs on the album and the specific effects Frusciante applied to bring their colors to life, the guitarist began with the album's lead-off single by explaining that on

'Dani California,' I used a straight Strat tone on the first section of the first verse, and on the second section the guitar signal is split and panned in stereo, with the original part on the left, and a part processed using my Doepfer modular synth on the right. Basically, the signal from the tape is used to trigger an envelope generator or ADSR, which responds to playing dynamics, and uses that information to dynamically control a low-pass filter. Unlike a typical envelope filter pedal, this setup allows me to create many more sounds than mere wah effects. Then, those two sections are repeated, and as I'm hanging on the sustained chord which transitions into the chorus, a Mellotron string part slowly rises behind the guitar. You can hardly hear the Mellotron, but it's what makes it feel like something really big is about to happen. On the chorus, I doubled the guitar parts, which were played using a Boss DS-2 Turbo Distortion pedal…The second verse begins with a couple of guitars playing in harmony. After they were recorded, I ran them through a Moog MF-105 MuRF Multiple Resonance Filter Array pedal six times, and recorded the results on individual tracks. The MuRF is very unpredictable, and sounded different on each pass. I kept going until I got a take that I really liked, though we actually wound up using all six takes in combination. Otherwise, the processing is the same as on the first verse…For the bridge, the rhythm guitar is processed with the Doepfer's LFO Low-Frequency Oscillator controlling its high-pass filter, so that the filter opens and closes rhythmically. The drums are also filtered, so that they are small and panned to one side at the beginning, then gradually get bigger and pan out across the full stereo spectrum, which lets you hear the guitar treatment more clearly...On the third verse I overdubbed an additional rhythm guitar track. Then, on the buildup to the chorus, I added some diminished chords along with several harmony parts.

To get the highest harmonies, we slowed the tape down and recorded them at a slower speed, so that they would be pitched above the range of the guitar when the tape was sped back up...There are lots of additional harmony guitar parts on the second half of the third chorus, positioned in two groups panned to either side. Also, Eddie Kramer came in and showed our engineer how to do 60s-style tape phasing, which we used on an early mix, and we wound up splicing a section of that mix into the part transitioning out of the chorus...I played the original solo when we recorded the basic tracks, and then doubled it later, except for the super-fast wah part at the end, which was too difficult to double perfectly, so I put that section through a Delta Labs Effectron II digital delay set to a quick delay with just a touch of slow modulation.

Engineer Ryan Hewitt, recalled,

at the end, it goes into that guitar solo...Well, John wanted to double-track it, so it was a bigger, thicker sound. So really, there are two guitars playing at that point. And he did that solo in one take. The solo you hear on the record is the solo he played in the room, with the band— that was one take, done. And then he went in to double it. He listened to it a couple of times and played it exactly the same. Again, in maybe two takes. It was perfectly similar—or as perfect as you can get... When you listen to 'Dani California',' the guitars are always changing, and there's all these effects going on, created with the modular synthesizer after he played them...So you have this endless palette to choose from to make those sounds, and John would never use the same sound twice. That was real exciting. At times, we would record the guitars at a different speed, so we'd change the speed of the tape so when he was listening to it, it was going really slow or really fast—at least compared to its normal speed. Then, when you play it back, it's like this totally different sound. At the end of 'Wet Sand,' it sounds like there's a harpsichord when really it's three guitars playing the harmony to each other at twice the tape speed.

Continuing, the guitarist explained that for *Stadium Arcadium,*

on the solo, we flipped the tape over and ran the sound through a vintage EMT 250 digital reverb, recording the reverb onto a separate track, so that when the tape was flipped back over the reverb would be reversed and begin just ahead of the guitar. Then, we ran the reverb sound through a low-pass filter—which lets you nail any sound down to the tiniest little sliver of a frequency—so that you not only hear the notes coming up ahead of the unprocessed guitar, they are swirling around, and the sound seemingly comes out of nothingness. Also, on the second verse, we slowed down the tape, and I picked some triads really fast, then we ran that sound through the EMT 250, which made them sound like futuristic mandolins from outer space...The effect on *Stadium Arcadium*and... 'C'mon Girl'...I turned the band upside-down. We had that old numeric reverb of 1976, the MT250, the very first one created actually. We passed my guitar in it, before sending it in a high frequency filter. When everything was at its maximum, the sound of the guitar was inaudible. Then, when I turned the frequencies button to the left, the sound of my guitar came back, starting by the most high-pitched frequencies. I recorded several tracks, and I only kept those that sounded the best.

Elaborating further, Frusciante recalled that

> on 'Strip My Mind'…the melodies in the second verse are
> two guitars playing in harmony, processed through an Ana-
> logue Systems Phase Shifter, which unlike a typical phase
> shifter has a really wide range, as well as a Resonance con-
> trol. When you run two or more harmony lines through it,
> and adjust the resonance really slowly by hand, at one fre-
> quency it will favor one note and its harmonics, and at
> another frequency it will favor another, with the whole
> thing moving in a circular fashion. And, sometimes when
> three notes are playing together, a fourth 'note' is created
> out of the combined frequencies and harmonics. I did the
> same thing on '*She Looks to Me*,' but there it was with
> chords rather than single notes. On the solo I used Elec-
> tro-Harmonix Big Muff Pi fuzz and Holy Grail reverb
> pedals. Rick Rubin really cranked the first note of the solo
> to give it a thunderous quality when it comes in…On '*War-
> locks*'… there's a cycle of two bars at the top of the second
> verse where I used a technique inspired by David Byrne and
> Brian Eno. You put notes in little spaces where you think,
> rhythmically, that there's a hole for a note, on four or five
> separate tracks. And though there is no conscious intent, all
> the notes taken together create a pattern. Then, I ran those
> parts through the MuRF, which randomly emphasized cer-
> tain notes, making them sound as if they are just breathing
> out, and not being picked. I really love that moment.

Turning to another of the album's tracks, Frusciante recalled,

> on 'She Looks to Me,' the three harmony guitars at the
> end were done using the English Muff'n, and then run
> through the Analogue Systems phaser and mixed to two
> tracks panned hard right and left. Normally when sounds
> are moving from speaker to speaker you hear exactly where
> they are at any given moment, but with this process cer-
> tain notes come out on the left that might or might not

come out on the right. Because the frequency of the phasing is moving so slowly, it creates a calming effect. Also, the two-note phrases on the verses were done by recording each note on its own track, then flipping the tape and adding reversed reverb to just the first note of each phrase. There's also an organ-like sound on the second chorus that's done with the POG... For 'Make You Feel Better', the overdubs on the final verse and chorus were played on a Les Paul, with the original panned left and a slightly out-of-time echo on the right. This was one of the last overdubs on the record, but I felt that it took the ending up to another level.

Frusciante also remembered that

on 'We Believe,' we used the Doepfer's LFO controlling its filter on the main guitar part, and there are also some harmony feedback tracks run through the MuRF on the opening to the second verse. I doubled Flea's bass line at the end with a Les Paul. The solo at the end was done using the English Muff'n, and treated afterwards with a DOD Analog Delay, the feedback knob of which I turned manually to get a controlled echo feedback thing... And on 'Death of a Martian'...the main guitar part was played through a Leslie, and the 'Martian' sounds were made with a filter that was modulated super-fast. There are three lead guitars on the outro, but they are mixed very quietly. On early Funkadelic albums, George Clinton would mess around with the volume of things, and not just have the parts fit into a perfectly balanced unity the way most producers do. On one track there would be really loud lead guitars, and on another super-loud bass, or quiet lead vocals, etc. The band and our producer were not into that as a general direction for the album, but this is one of the few spots where I'm doing that sort of thing... Another thing I did on this album, which comes in a little on that track, is tape speed manipulation. The idea with that solo was to have a lot of guitars coming in and out, and that was one of the few sections I mixed myself. There were so many tracks of solos, the engineer had no idea what to do with them so I went in and figured out how I wanted them to be orchestrated. There are five cycles in 2 minutes and I approached each section differently, with regards as to which guitar to feature. I did some Jimi Hendrix stuff where I turned things up and down with the faders while they were playing.

Another instrumental area Frusciante focused heavily on in the recording of the album was the presence of synthesizers utilized in unconventional manners in the studio:

this time, I treated my tracks with some effects, but after their recording, for example, I put them through a modular synthesizer. It was funny to do, because I could freely turn the buttons in every direction and I was focused on the music. To do so while playing, I should have four hands and two brains. I also used a numeric delay or the new Moogerfooger Murf pedal from Moog, which is really excellent…I love to reproduce that kind of sounds with my keyboards. People like Page or Hendrix made 'white noise,' while Randy Rhodes avoided it, and people used to imitate Rhodes because they believed that the essence of the guitar is playing it clean and fast. I also had to fight against that tendency of imitate Rhodes, because I told ya, I admired him, and I had to constantly keep in my mind that I had to mistreat the guitar and never worry about getting just clean tones. In this album, I tried to go by the production of Hendrix's albums. He's been my biggest inspiration. I wanted to reproduce that psychedelic effect he got by manipulating the speed of the tapes—where you hear an electric mandolin that's really a guitar taped in high speed, the manipulation of the volume, changing from one loudspeaker to another, playing faster or slower than the rest of the band, constantly changes in rhythm… In the song 'Animal Bar' for example, I use the pedals to create a guitar sound that sounds like a synthesizer. I don't usually use the pedals. Most of the times, when I have recorded the guitar parts, I pass them through the synthesizer and then I pass them to tape again…

…on 'Flea's Trumpet,' in the beginning and in the end of the second verse of 'Death of a Martian.' We can hear this pedal or the modular synthesizer on every song, but it's often very subtle. That's great, because there are not many subtle effects on the market. I did a lot of things by using the various signals. Sometimes, it sounds as if another guitarist plays with me. However, it is the same guitar. On the verses of '*Dani California*', there is the normal rhythm guitar that I play live, when there's part B, I send the sound in the modular synthesizer that I use as a dynamic filter. It opens and closes very quickly according to how I play the cords. I had fun; One of the things I am the proudest of is on '*Stadium Arcadium.*'… For this album, I did a lot of vocal harmony, I did a lot of guitar overdubs. Luckily, they all ended up serving the song really well, which was my original intention. When you're a guy that's just stuck in a room trying to write lyrics every day, you can't step outside yourself that far to see clearly where someone else is going. You've just got to trust. Luckily, we've got that trust and we always end up agreeing on everything but we don't always know we are going to agree on everything.

Addressing Anthony Kiedis' process for tracking vocals in the studio, drummer Chad Smith mused that "he's a mad scientist in the studio…and we let him do his thing." Frusciante also described the dynamic between the rest of the band during tracking, which as usual they did live off the floor. He first addressed Chad Smith's abilities as a studio drummer, explaining "he's great at being…tight but not rigid. I was especially pushing for lots of sections to be at slightly different tempos than other sections. Like in 'Dani California,' I really wanted the chorus to be slower than the verse, and Chad can do that. In the studio, we're always talking about how many 'clicks per minute' something is. Chad's really in control of that. We'll tell him 'just slow down two clicks,' and he can do it. It's something we all do together; we all feel the tempo in precise, scientific way."

Addressing his and Flea's synergy as players, Frusciante explained,

> Flea and I found our rhythmic connection on a deeper level on this album. As a result, there's a lot of tempo shifting, but it's in service of the song, and it's subtle enough that you probably don't even notice it…Riffing in unison is…something that comes naturally to us…I wrote the riff for 'Readymade' on bass. I'd been practicing bass 'cause I'd been listening to a lot of hip-hop music and a lot of those records use guitar samples; the only thing that's consistent throughout the song is the bass. So I'd be listening to the vocals for rhythmic ideas to use in my guitar playing, but I'd be seeing a theme in relationship to the bass. My mind would be working all the time on a polyrhythmic level, listening to what the MCs were doing, but my fingers would be in that straight bass pocket. So that's how 'Readymade' ended up being written on a bass…Flea and I were really getting inside each other's heads. For a long time, *BloodSugar* was our main point of reference, just in terms of the energy behind it. We'd ask, 'Is this new song or album standing up to what we did then?' The number-one ingredient that made *BloodSugar* great is that we were really playing along as people, for the most part…Flea and I have been influenced by Clapton and Bruce from Cream. We can play two totally different lines and still create an homogeneous dynamic, punch at rough state. We are so united… no need to show this cohesion by playing twin

riffs. It's better to play against each other and see how everything comes together. Everything comes together in the end.

Describing his process for tracking guitars past the rhythm parts he lays with the band live, Frusciante explained:

we composed and recorded the base tracks all together, then I worked alone. Anthony worked with Rick Rubin to record his vocal parts. I did my overdubs on my own, with a sound engineer and an assistant. I got all the time I needed to experiment, and I did so 12 to 14 hours a day. I love all those songs, and I wanted each of them to be perfectly completed. At the same time, my challenge was to create something I had never heard before. For that, my solo albums enabled me to use the studio in a creative way. The fact I used the same sound engineer who worked on my two last records helped me. He also mixed the Chili Peppers album. We gained by an experience we got working together, and we're faster today, 'cause we know how to get some sounds. There are only two songs on the album with keyboards. On every other one, it is guitar. When it sounds like a mix of melotron and mandolin, it's actually accelerated guitars. I did a lot of things by changing the speed of bands. On songs as 'Dani California,' 'Turn it again,' 'West sand,' 'Hard to concentrate,' and 'Stadium Arcadium,' there's a guitar or a group of guitars that are accelerated on the band. Actually, I recorded those parts with the song played slowly, then I put back the band at its normal speed. When you listen to it after that, the guitars sound completely differently.

Always the band's point man during mixing sessions, Frusciante pulled double-duty as a co-producer during mixing, explaining that, conceptually, he wanted to make a record that would be a sound experience for the listeners.

I wanted the music to put them in a trance and enter their subconscious, where all the sounds mix together and bring them to another world… The guys in the band all really believe in me. They're the ones who gave me the chance to go in all the different directions that I've gone. Besides, they get a certain kind of attention that I don't get, and there's no bad feelings about that either way. Their main concern is just preserving what we all fall in love with so much when we're in the rehearsal hall writing the songs. But in the end, the bottom line is that they trust me. I have no interest in taking away from the band. I wanted harmonies, I wanted overdubs, but I only wanted to do it if the band still sounded really raw. I would look back to Jimi Hendrix or Led Zeppelin records, or this band the Move, who really inspired me…Their records sound really raw. The bass is awesome the drums are really strong, but there's a lot of guitar overdubs and harmonies and sonic effects going on…Our style of mixing sort of prohibited me from having the drums, guitar and bass all coming up and down in volume all the time like on *Electric Ladyland*. But at least my guitars are in constant state of movement…I was constantly taking what was on tape, running it through the modular and putting that back onto tape.

Transitioning from the tracking phase into that of mixing, the guitarist felt that the move was

a bit fast between the end of the mix and the release of the album. It's a bit my fault, I wanted to take a lot of time to perfect the production. I recorded a lot of backing vocals, guitars overdubs, electronic treatments… I knew that the mix couldn't be finished in two days! We had to find a compromise—Anthony wanted to release the album last fall, I wanted to take my time…We had a little tension before the mixing started because Flea thought he was going to want it different than me. Anthony thought he was going to want it different. It ended up that once we mixed the first song, we realized that everybody was liking the same thing. But it is this huge pressure when you've gone as far as I've gone…I thought I was going to come up against a lot of resistance to what I was doing with the mixes. My vision for the album was to retain all the raw power of the band playing live in the studio but also to have additional guitars and sonic effects enhancing what was already there. But on the rough mixes it didn't really sound like that, so there was a lot of tension building, because some people though, 'Oh, John's going overdub crazy,' or 'He's turning it into a Beach Boys album.' The main problem was that we'd been listening to the band's basic tracks on a slave. It was transferred badly, so the mix sounded really dull, while the overdubs were much brighter. That was freaking people out. But when we synced up the overdubs on the slave reel to the original 24-track master eel, everything sounded awesome. It's not that the overdubs ended up being softer; it was that the band sounded so much burlier. So we all ended up loving the final mixes. There hasn't been a single instance of somebody not wanting to use something that I'd done. It all ended up serving the song well. So that was cool… Some of these songs have 71 channels that they are using on the board…That's 71 different things to be balancing. I had a whole 24-track machine just for my backing vocals and a whole 24-track machine just for the guitar overdubs and another 24-track machine for the band. We had three 24-track machines going at once for these songs, so they are a real job to mix.

Aside perhaps from Rick Rubin, Frusciante cited his main influence concerning his preferences for mixing as a music legend that surprised no one who knew the guitar player's historic influences: "I have been influenced by Hendrix for his guitar play, but mostly for his producer talents. We often forget about it, but *Electric Ladyland* is the world's greatly mixed album! A material constantly moving, where you can physically feel the symbiosis between the three instruments…The speakers become alive. Hendrix was an artist of the sound who was creating gigantic sound orgasms. It's an infinite source of knowledge and the creation of Stadium owes him a lot. For me, playing guitar doesn't mean hitting some strings and move my fingers on the guitar. Since *BloodSugar*, I learn to think less in terms of notes or technique and more of sounds and texture." Frusciante seemed particularly relieved when mixing was finally completed, explaining that mixing the album was a drag because it's not a very creative process. "But now that its done…I can meditate and practice more now. I can take walks in the sunshine now."

Once principle tracking and mixing was finished, according to singer Anthony Kiedis, the toughest part of the recording process was "cutting down the tracks…which…was excruciating…But we did it in a very scientific way, where everyone was involved in and petitioned for the ones they thought should make it onto the record. It was along process and everyone had to suffer a bit. There was too much democracy!" Flea recalled that the length of the album was "especially ironic when you consider that we set out to write a classic 12-song record… We said, 'We always have too many songs. We gotta keep it concise this time.' But we can't stop writing once we get going. Everybody's ideas were encouraged and turned into songs. We were really working well together and on top of our games individually."

Describing his favorite moments on the results they attained in the studio, Kiedis explained that "it's definitely a body of work that fits together very naturally…There's still a lot of vocal harmonies on there too…Our old school fans are always getting at us, asking if we're going to go back to funk again, here where those elements are more pronounced… There's some retardedly painful funk on this record. There are a few songs that are just straight-up dirty funk, and beyond that I think there are many songs that will surprise our fans…There is a weird thread that connects back to our first three records…There's this weird kind of sublime, subliminal undercurrent that is suggestive, in a spirited way, of our earliest records." Commenting on the results the band had achieved in context of their future creative direction, engineer Andy Schepps felt that "to me, *By the Way* seemed to be the first record in whatever direction they were going, and *Stadium Arcadium* is where they're starting to realize it…It's less grooves and more songs, and Anthony is just singing his ass off…And now he's a great singer. They were doing more of the same, but they were a lot more confident at it because they'd been doing it for a while, and they were just better at it. It seems as though this could be—and it's ridiculous, because they have been making records for so long—but this could be the beginning of the next set of records they make."

With *Stadium Arcadium*, many felt the Red Hot Chili Peppers had finally come full-circle creatively. It had taken them 25 years and nine studio albums to produce what was perhaps their most rounded album musically in terms of the number of derivative styles it incorporated and new genres the band expanded into in the course of its expansive 28 tracks. The album was so musically accomplished it won a record seven Grammy Awards in 2007, including 'Rock Album of the Year' among others. As *Rolling Stone Magazine* saw things, "much of the credit for the album's depth—and the swelling, ever-morphing, headphone-candy arrangements that boost every track—goes to the band's not-so-secret weapon,

John Frusciante. It's been clear since his return to the band on 1999's *Californication* that Frusciante came away from his near-fatal heroin addiction with new musical superpowers, and they're in full bloom on *Stadium Arcadium*."

His bandmates, beginning with vocalist Anthony Kiedis, was equally as complimentary of the guitarist's contributions to the album: "the artistic center of his brain is pretty much all of his brain." Flea, for his part, hailed Frusciante as "the greatest musician in the world." Critical praise wasn't merely reserved for the guitarist however. *Rolling Stone Magazine* further concluding in its review of the album that "Flea has spent years whittling down his frantic popping and slapping to a Zen-like melodic minimalism, while melding ever more deeply with Chad Smith, who remains the swingingest rock drummer this side of Mitch Mitchell. But after 2002's *By the Way*, the band's least funky album, the bassist finally cuts loose again here, reasserting himself as the best non-hip-hop reason to buy a subwoofer."

Continuing with its glowing praise for the band's artistic growth, the magazine pointed to "Anthony Kiedis, whose vocals keep improving at an age when many rockers start slipping their high notes to backup singers. He shows versatility throughout…Kiedis is also, more or less, the inventor of rap rock, and he embraces his roots, dropping the most rhymes on any album since *BloodSugarSexMagik*. He hasn't updated his flow in a couple of decades… but the very familiarity of the style makes it an appealing counterpoint to the band's latter-day melodic splendor, instead of a Durst-ian embarrassment."

Seeming satisfied at the end of the day with the depths and heights they had traveled as a band in the course the sonic adventure that was *Stadium Arcadium*, guitarist John Frusciante remarked that "there's heavier stuff than the band's ever done, and there's also a lot of beautiful, soaring melodies…I feel like everybody's taking their instrument to a new level…I feel bad for people when I see that they can't change…The only reason I'm interested in being in a band with Flea and Anthony is because they're more open-minded now;

they're into going to any lengths to be different from what we've done in the past." Flea, for his part, felt that "we worked really hard and focused in…I'm very in love with this record." As for Anthony Kiedis, he concluded that the band's latest studio opus was "the best thing that we've ever done, and I just want to get it out there on the airwaves and in the earholes of the world."

Fans and critics alike were avid listeners and lovers of the band's latest—and many argued—greatest studio opus to date, with the band's home-town paper, the *L.A. Times,* for one of many, observing in its review of the band's latest double-LP that it "overflows with the kind of music the Chili Peppers do best: a physical, often psychedelic mix of spastic bass-slapped funk and glistening alt-rock spiritualism. Only they've never sounded this good as musicians." In further recognizing the band's maturity musically, *Billboard Magazine* declared in its review that "the message is loud and clear: twenty-three years into their career, the Red Hot Chili Peppers sound euphoric and enormously alive. *Stadium Arcadium* is a mature showcase of concentrated power with riotous groove jams, super-sized hooks and transcendent vocal arrangements…One wild melodic rush…Rick Rubin's airy production squeezes the essence out of a monster—without taming it…The Peppers' strongest set since *BloodSugarSexMagik.*" *Entertainment Weekly,* for its part, celebrated being "blindsided by how great it all sounds," and summarized that "*Stadium Arcadium* ensures that graying Lollapalooza-era fans, indie teens, and rowdy lunkheads will all be satisfied." *Q Magazine* concluded that the album "represents a career high," while *Mojo Magazine* jovially hailed "the sound of a band on a roll."

Conclusion

2008 & Beyond

With 25 years and nine studio albums to their credit, the Red Hot Chili Peppers are still years and countless hit singles and new musical revolutions away from rounding out their legacy. Still, they have come full-circle in terms of defining their own subgenre of rock, one that has played a pivotal role in influencing several waves of multi-platinum rock bands. In assessing the latter, singer Anthony Kiedis agreed that they were definitely part of that first wave. Meanwhile, bandmate and bassist Flea added "I think you can definitely make a case for us being a big part of what became Nu-Metal or Rap Rock/Metal…So when I meet those bands that are along that rap metal vein—Nu-Metal or whatever you want to call it—they often say they enjoyed us when they were beginning."

Elaborating on the latter in modern terms, Flea feels that "sometimes I hear music that we've influenced and think it's being taken to a great place. Other times I think people only see the superficial aspects of our band. I influenced a lot of white rock bassists with my athletic-style playing. After our last record, all these long-haired metal guys started coming to our shows, and now it's turned into this whole fast slap-a-thon." In offering perhaps the oddest case of the band's sound influencing another rock artist, guitarist John Frusciante recalled, "Axl Rose told us that Guns 'N Roses had the Chili Peppers in mind when they did 'Rocket Queen.'" Clearly, the Chili Peppers are no longer merely stars; the band is now its own planet in a rock's greater galaxy.

Having maintained a bond with one another musically and personally that carried them through countless miles of trials and tribulations as a band, the Red Hot Chili Peppers' also have remained with long-time producer Rick Rubin. Anthony Kiedis explains, "I talk to Rick almost every day of my life…He really has earned his place as the producer of this band. He has improved his game consistently. He just gets better and better and he's willing to work harder and harder. His intuition flourishes." With the common musical aim in mind of maturing as a band on each record they have made, as well as those musical frontiers the pair has yet to explore, the world is sure to be watching and listening.

In underscoring the band's continued vitality, consider the *New York Times'* conclusion that the band "brims with a creative euphoria almost shocking for a band that has been around since Ronald Reagan's first term." *The Village Voice* has summarized the band in legacy terms as "firmly ensconced in the upper echelon of modern rock stardom," while they in the same time have noted that "the Red Hot Chili Peppers have now set upon securing a spot in the pantheon." Aided by their former-mentioned status, and with an arena packed with thousands upon thousands of devoted musical disciples in countless cities around the world, the band's temple is already well under construction. Based alone on the Red Hot Chili Peppers' 25 years in the studio, the foundation is already cemented, as is the band's permanent place in broader rock history.

Photo Gallery
Red Hot Chili Peppers
Live Performances

Anthony Keidis: Vocals (1983-Present)

Chad Smith: Drums, Percussion (1988-Present

Flea (Michael Balgary): Bass Guitar (1983-Present)

John Frusciante: Guitar, Vocals
(1988-1992; 1998-Present)

Red Hot Chili Peppers
Chart History & Awards

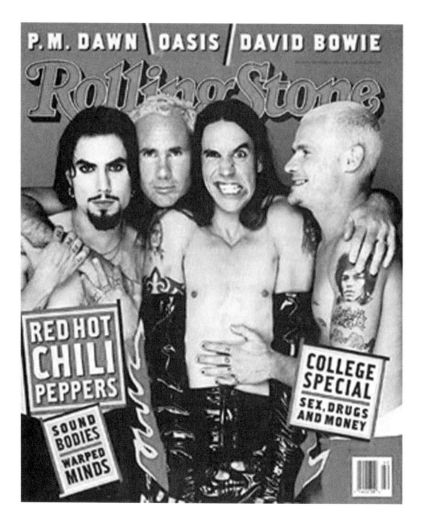

Chart History
Studio Albums/Singles:

Title: *The Red Hot Chili Peppers*
Released: 1983
Chart positions: N/A
RIAA certification: Platinum
Worldwide sales: 1,000,000
Singles: N/A

Title: *Freaky Styley*
Released: 1985
Chart positions: N/A
RIAA certification: Platinum
Worldwide sales: Platinum
Singles: N/A

Title: *The Abbey Road E.P.*
Released: 1986
Chart positions: N/A
RIAA certification: Gold (500,000)
Worldwide sales: Platinum (1,000,000)
Singles: N/A

Title: *Uplift Mojo Party Plan*
Released: 1987
Chart positions: 148
RIAA certification: Gold (500,000)
Worldwide sales: 750,000
Singles: 'Me & My Friends,' 'Behind the Sun,' 'Fight Like a Brave'

Title: *Mother's Milk*
Released: 1989
Chart positions: 52
RIAA certification: 2,000,000
Worldwide sales: 3,000,000
Singles: 'Knock Me Down', # 6 on Billboard's US Modern Rock Singles Chart, 'Higher Ground', # 11 on Billboard's US Modern Rock Singles Chart, 'Taste the Pain'

Title: *BloodSugarSexMagik*
Released: 1991
Chart positions: 3
RIAA certification: 7 x Platinum
Worldwide sales: 12 x Platinum
Singles: 'Give It Away', # 1 on Billboard's US Modern Rock Singles
Chart, 'Under the Bridge', # 2 on Billboard's US Hot 100 Singles
Chart, # 2 on Billboard's US Modern Rock Singles Chart, 'Suck My
Kiss,' # 15 on Billboard's US Modern Rock Singles Chart, 'Breaking the
Girl,' # 19 on Billboard's US Modern Rock Singles Chart

Title: **What Hits?**
Released: 1992
Chart positions: 22
RIAA certification: 1.5 million
Worldwide sales: 2.5 million
Singles: 'Soul to Squeeze,' # 22 on Billboard's US Modern Rock Singles
Chart, # 1 on Billboard's US Modern Rock Singles Chart

Title: **One Hot Minute**
Released: 1995
Chart positions: 4
RIAA certification: 2 x Platinum
Worldwide sales: 5 x Platinum
Singles: 'Warped,' # 7 on Billboard's US Modern Rock Singles Chart,
'My Friends,' # 1 on Billboard's US Modern Rock Singles Chart, 'Aero-
plane,' # 8 on Billboard's US Modern Rock Singles Chart

Title: **Californication**
Released: 1999
Chart positions: 3
RIAA certification: 6 x Platinum
Worldwide sales: 15 x Platinum
Singles: 'Scar Tissue', # 6 on Billboard's US Hot 100 Singles Chart, # 1
on Billboard's US Modern Rock Singles Chart, 'Californication,' # 1 on
Billboard's US Modern Rock Singles Chart, 'Around the World,' # 7 on
Billboard's US Modern Rock Singles Chart, 'The Other Side,' # 14 on
Billboard's US Hot 100 Singles Chart, # 1 on Billboard's US Modern
Rock Singles Chart

Title: *By the Way*
Released: 2002
Chart position: # 2
RIAA certification: 2 x Platinum
Worldwide sales: 9 x Platinum
Singles: 'By the Way,' #34 on # 6 on Billboard's US Hot 100 Singles
Chart, # 1 on Billboard's US Modern Rock Singles Chart, 'The Zephyr
Song,' # 49 on Billboard's US Hot 100 Singles Chart, # 6 on Billboard's
US Modern Rock Singles Chart, 'Can't Stop,' # 1 on Billboard's US
Modern Rock Singles Chart

Title: *Greatest Hits*
Released: 2003
Chart positions: 18
RIAA certification: 2 x Platinum
Worldwide sales: 4 x Platinum
Singles: N/A

Title: *Stadium Arcadium*
Released: 2006
Chart position: 1
RIAA certification: 3 x Platinum
Worldwide sales: 8 x Platinum
Singles: 'Dani California,' # 6 on Billboard's Hot 100 Singles Chart, # 1
on Billboard's US Modern Rock Singles Chart, 'Tell Me Baby,' # 1 on
Billboard's US Modern Rock Singles Chart, 'Snow (Hey Oh)', # 22 on
Billboard's US Hot 100 Singles Chart, # 1 on Billboard's US Modern
Rock Singles Chart, 'Hump de Bump,' # 8 on Billboard's US Modern
Rock Singles Chart

Awards History:

Year	Award	Title
1992	MTV VMA—Breakthrough Video	"Give It Away"
1992	MTV VMA—Viewer's Choice	"Under the Bridge"
1993	Grammy Awards—Best Hard Rock Perf.	"Give It Away"
2000	MTV VMA—Video Vanguard (Career)	
2000	Billboard Awards—Best Alternative Group	
2000	American Music Awards—Favorite Alternative Artist	
2000	Grammy Awards—Best Rock Song	"Scar Tissue"
2006	American Music Awards—Favorite Alternative Artist	
2007	Grammy Awards—Best Rock Performance by Group w/Vocal	"Dani Cali."
2007	Grammy Awards—Best Rock Song	"Dani California"
2007	Grammy Awards—Best Rock Album	"Stadium Arcadium"
2007	Grammy Awards—Best Producer (Rick Rubin)	"Stadium Arcadium"

About the Author

Nashville-based music biographer **Jake Brown** is the author of fifteen published books, including *Black Eyed Peas: The Unauthorized Biography*; *Dr. Dre: In the Studio*; *Kanye West In The Studio: Beats Down! Money Up! (The Studio Years (2000-2006)*; *Tupac Shakur (2-Pac) In the Studio: The Studio Years (1987-1996)*; *50 Cent: No Holds Barred*; *Jay Z and the Roc-A-Fella Dynasty; Ready to Die: The Story of Biggie Smalls—Notorious B.I.G.; Your Body's Calling Me: The Life and Times of Robert "R" Kelly—Music, Love, Sex & Money;* and *Suge Knight: The Rise, Fall and Rise of Death Row Records*. Brown was also a featured author in Rick James' recently published autobiography, *Memoirs of a Super Freak: The Confessions of Rick James*. Brown is also owner of the hard rock label Versailles Records.

ORDER FORM

WWW.AMBERBOOKS.COM

Fax Orders: 480-283-0991
Telephone Orders: 480-460-1660
Postal Orders: Send Checks & Money Orders to:
    Amber Books
    1334 E. Chandler Blvd., Suite 5-D67, Phoenix, AZ 85048
Online Orders: E-mail: Amberbk@aol.com

_____*Red Hot Chili Peppers: In the Studio*, ISBN #: 978-0-9790976-5-2, $16.95
_____*Black Eyed Peas: Unauthorized Biography*, ISBN 978-0-9790976-4-5, $16.95
_____*Dr. Dre In the Studio*, ISBN#: 0-9767735-5-4, $16.95
_____*Kanye West in the Studio*, ISBN #: 0-9767735-6-2, $16.95
_____*Tupac Shakur—(2Pac) In The Studio*, ISBN#: 0-9767735-0-3, $16.95
_____*Jay-Z…and the Roc-A-Fella Dynasty*, ISBN#: 0-9749779-1-8, $16.95
_____*Your Body's Calling Me: The Life & Times of "Robert" R. Kelly*, ISBN#: 0-9727519-5-52, $16.95
_____*Ready to Die: Notorious B.I.G.*, ISBN#: 0-9749779-3-4, $16.95
_____*Suge Knight: The Rise, Fall, and Rise of Death Row Records*, ISBN#: 0-9702224-7-5, $21.95
_____*50 Cent: No Holds Barred*, ISBN#: 0-9767735-2-X, $16.95
_____*Aaliyah—An R&B Princess in Words and Pictures* , ISBN#: 0-9702224-3-2, $10.95
_____*You Forgot About Dre: Dr. Dre & Eminem*, ISBN#: 0-9702224-9-1, $10.95
_____*Divas of the New Millenium*, ISBN#: 0-9749779-6-9, $16.95
_____*Michael Jackson: The King of Pop*, ISBN#: 0-9749779-0-X, $29.95
_____*The House that Jack Built (Hal Jackson Story)*, ISBN#: 0-9727519-4-7, $16.95

Name:_____

Company Name:_____

Address:_____

City:_____State:_____Zip:_____

Telephone: (____) _____E-mail:_____

For Bulk Rates Call: **480-460-1660**   **ORDER NOW**

Red Hot Chili Peppers	$16.95	❑ Check ❑ Money Order ❑ Cashiers Check
Black Eyed Peas	$16.95	❑ Credit Card: ❑ MC ❑ Visa ❑ Amex ❑ Discover
Dr. Dre In the Studio	$16.95	
Kanye West	$16.95	
Tupac Shakur	$16.95	CC#_____
Jay-Z…	$16.95	Expiration Date:_____
Your Body's Calling Me:	$16.95	**Payable to:**
Ready to Die: Notorious B.I.G.,	$16.95	Amber Books
Suge Knight:	$21.95	1334 E. Chandler Blvd., Suite 5-D67
50 Cent: No Holds Barred,	$16.95	Phoenix, AZ 85048
Aaliyah—An R&B Princess	$10.95	
Dr. Dre & Eminem	$10.95	**Shipping:** $5.00 per book. Allow 7 days for delivery.
Divas of the New Millenium,	$16.95	**Sales Tax:** Add 7.05% to books shipped to Arizona addresses.
Michael Jackson: The King of Pop	$29.95	
The House that Jack Built	$16.95	**Total enclosed: $**_____